PRICELESS

PRICELESS

*Beyond Customer Care
to Customer Delight*

CHARLES DECKER
and GENE FERENCE

PRICELESS
BEYOND CUSTOMER CARE TO CUSTOMER DELIGHT

iUniverse books may be ordered through booksellers or by contacting:

iUniverse
1663 Liberty Drive
Bloomington, IN 47403
www.iuniverse.com
1-800-Authors (1-800-288-4677)

ISBN: 978-1-4917-5242-5 (sc)
ISBN: 978-1-4917-5244-9 (hc)
ISBN: 978-1-4917-5243-2 (e)

Library of Congress Control Number: 2014919643

Printed in the United States of America.

iUniverse rev. date: 11/25/2014

To J. J. D., for making the journey more interesting than the destination

Contents

Foreword

As employees, many of us have worked in different types of service organizations—some good, some excellent, and some downright awful. What makes the difference? Why is one hotel highly recommended while another is not even considered? Why do you see one restaurant full of satisfied diners and the one next door empty? Why do we prefer to shop at one store with higher prices and not at its low-cost competitor? The answer is often that elusive and multidimensional term "customer service."

But the standards of service evolve from creating an organizational culture, and developing organizational cultures is a process. Unlike a single event, a process never stops. Seeking to achieve excellence and organizational peak performance has become the challenge for everyone working in the service sector. Clear vision, mission, core values, standards, and systems form the strategic foundation of the organization's long-term success. But it's the minute-by-minute teamwork, engagement, and passion in providing all of the products, services, and experiences that make the difference in achieving what the authors of this short but powerful book call "customer delight."

Most organizations "talk" customer service and put it at the top of their to-do list but then fail to walk the talk when it comes to training and development programs. Many of those programs only give employees a uniform checklist for what to do in myriad situations while hoping the one-size-fits-all approach will work.

Few provide long-term, interactive, behavioral tools to further employees' understanding and skills. *Priceless: Beyond Customer Care to Customer Delight* provides a new and dynamic format for readers. This book is a business fable designed to offer a nonthreatening approach to creating a better world of service. Embedded in the story are two different situations—hotels in different locations at very different points on the success scale, real-world personalities intertwined in the web of creating service delight, and thought-provoking questions designed to generate discussion with fellow team members.

Every service organization faces challenges in the areas of satisfaction and engagement. Differing points of view regarding communication, empowerment, motivation, interactions, teamwork, and passion form the foundation for human dynamics. In *Priceless*, you and your team will be able to dig into core issues and address them in realistic ways using your own organizational culture as the point of reference.

Priceless is designed to be read, discussed, and acted upon. True customer delight comes from understanding your present culture, gaining agreement on changes needed to raise the level of service, and developing action plans in the pursuit of achieving the very best of product, service, and experience. All this can only be accomplished with—and through—others. *Priceless* has been written to encourage everyone to dialogue about their work environment and, more importantly, share success stories and learnings from a variety of sources and experiences.

To do this:

- Set aside time in meetings (department, training, preshift) to discuss and work through each chapter's group discussion questions found at the end of every chapter. They are designed to provide a framework for lively conversations.

- Gain insights, observations, and experiences from your fellow team members. Ask questions, share successes, and allow yourself to be open to others' personal histories.
- Establish new goals that will complement your continuous improvement initiatives.
- Ask yourself how you personally can play a more active role in the success of your team and the organization overall.
- Follow up and follow through.

As you read this book, remember that no situation is entirely unique; every situation, no matter the outcome, can include learnings that we often can't predict. Open your mind to the fact that the way you personally approach your job and your customer can very much impact how that interaction turns out. Set the bar high and constantly strive to surpass it.

Giving customers the service they expect—well done.

Turning customer service into something memorable—superb.

Combining memorable experiences to create customer delight—*priceless*.

—Horst Schulze,
President and COO,
The West Paces Hotel Group;
Former President and COO,
Ritz-Carlton Hotels

Authors' Note

The following is a work of fiction, but it is based on extensive research at two hotels on both coasts of the United States. Some of the characters are composites, and the time frame has been compressed.

PART ONE

Chapter 1

Strangers on a Train

There is never enough time—unless you're serving it.
—Malcolm Forbes

Sprinting to make her train, Cora Tyler thought she might actually miss it and have to explain her chronic tardiness yet again. Though she was famously (or infamously) late, this time, in her mind, it wasn't her fault. Well, it was ... but it wasn't. She had spent most of the week attending a hotel convention in Washington, DC, and had forgotten about daylight saving time beginning that crisp March morning. "Spring forward; fall back." *A good hotel would have reminded me*, she thought.

She climbed onto the train just as the conductor announced, "All aboard." She knew from working in the travel industry that the late-Sunday-afternoon Acela Express from Washington to New York was almost always crowded, but this train seemed packed to the gills. *Where am I going to put my suitcase?* she wondered, surveying the overheads.

"There's more space in the next car forward," the conductor said, noticing the concerned look on her face. "And it's not as warm up there either."

Cora thanked him and hauled her purse and suitcase and the enormous bag of materials she had picked up at the hotel convention into the next car. She spotted an aisle seat midcar and noticed there was space in the overhead as well. Lifting the suitcase and the heavy bag of literature was a struggle, but she managed. Her seatmate tried to offer some help, but she thanked him and waved him off. She sat down and exhaled. She realized that even on this cool almost-spring day, she was perspiring. Pulling out a packet of lavender-scented tissues, she began dabbing her forehead.

"Just relax," her seatmate said reassuringly. "You made the train. That's the most important thing. And now you have four hours to do nothing."

"I wish!" Cora said. "I have plenty to do. But first I have to call my cousins in New Jersey and tell them about missing the earlier train. I totally forgot about daylight saving time."

"Oh, that happened to me once too," her seatmate said. "I actually almost missed seeing a matinee of *Hairspray* on Broadway because of it. I saw the second act at least. Edna Turnblad had already gotten made over by then. That's always been one of my favorite movies, so I was dying to see the musical. Did you?"

"Strangely enough, I actually saw the very first performance of that musical when I was visiting some friends in Seattle. Did you know it started in Seattle?"

"Why would you see it in Seattle when you knew it was coming to Broadway?"

"Oh, I don't live in New York; I live in San Francisco. My name's Cora, by the way. Seems I always talk to people on planes and trains and never get to know their names."

"And mine's Ari. I agree. I am pretty gregarious by nature, as you can probably already tell, but it seems people are kind of protective about exchanging names."

Cora pulled out her bottle of Dasani water and took a gulp. She was still overheated.

"You know," Cora began, "I work in a hotel, and on our first day of training, the manager hammered into us how important it is to call people by their given names, so I try to remember that in daily life as well. It just makes it all so much more personal. On the job, we are constantly reminded to develop positive relations with guests as soon as possible. We use the ten-foot-zone rule: make meaningful eye contact within ten feet of the person; smile in a sincere and friendly manner within five feet; extend a warm, enthusiastic greeting; and use the person's name if possible." *There I go running my mouth again,* she thought.

Ari smiled. "That's funny. I work in a hotel too. But I couldn't even pronounce most of our guests' names. I guess in San Francisco you mostly deal with Americans, right?"

"No, not always," Cora answered. "We have a lot of Asians and a lot of Spanish-speaking people too. That's probably why they hired me."

"Why? Are you Asian? You don't look it."

"Well, I'm sort of a mutt. I was born in the Philippines and grew up speaking both English and Spanish, as well as a little Tagalog. Some people think I am Asian. I kind of like being perceived as a little bit *exotic*. What about you? Ari is a pretty unusual name for an American. The only other Ari I've heard of was married to Jackie

Kennedy—and he was Greek. You *are* American, right? You don't have any sort of accent."

"Oh, I guess you could say I'm a mutt too, though my parents would probably be highly offended. I am Israeli by birth but consider myself totally assimilated now."

The conductor arrived to collect their tickets. Cora realized hers was in the overstuffed convention literature bag above. She rose from her seat to retrieve it.

"Just a second," she told the conductor, fumbling with the training and sales materials she had collected. "I know it's here somewhere. All this rushing has made me scattered." Finding it, she exclaimed, "Oh, here it is, here it is."

She handed the conductor the mangled ticket that she had bought seconds before the train departed. She wasn't even sure she had chosen the right destination. The whole morning seemed like a blur to her.

"Newark, right?" the conductor asked. "One way?"

"That would be a yes to both," Cora answered. "I missed the earlier train because of the time change. When do you think I could make a call on my phone to tell my family I'm going to be late?"

"You can do it now, though there's a tunnel coming up so I would suggest you wait until after that if you're planning on talking for a while. Probably another three or four minutes."

"I need to make a call too," Ari said. "I promise to try and make it short. I hate people talking on their cell phones in public. Totally rude, I think."

"I agree completely. I just have to call my cousins to tell them I am going to be an hour late. They offered to pick me up in Newark. It won't take long. Besides, I'm enjoying talking to you. So, I'm assuming you live in New York, right? It must be so exciting."

"Yeah, it is. It's also probably the easiest place in the country to be Jewish."

"There are lots of Jews in San Francisco, too, you know. You don't have a corner on the market!"

Ari chuckled. He was enjoying this woman's banter.

"Oh, I know that. But it's something you have to consider when you're Jewish. Do you have a large Jewish clientele in your hotel?"

Cora took a moment to reflect. She didn't really know the answer to such a question.

"That is something I probably have never thought about, Ari. We welcome people from everywhere. It's a beautiful and wonderfully run boutique hotel that people seem to love, even though it's not at all fancy. I really enjoy working there. It's called the Hotel Metronome. Maybe you've heard of it? Even though it's on Nob Hill, it's not stuffy in the least. We call it a *lifestyle hotel* now."

"That's another amazing coincidence. Our hotel is called the Metro! And it couldn't even *pretend* to be stuffy—let alone 'lifestyle,' whatever that means. I know envy is supposed to be one of the seven deadly sins, but I have to admit I am a little jealous of your situation. It seems like you are totally proud of your job, while I hate mine. I love people and I speak several languages, too, so I thought this would be the place that would value someone like me. The guests are penny-pinchers and often incredibly rude. Isn't it amazing how perfectly competent and intelligent people can become like whiny babies when they travel? In fact, people on vacation seem to think they have a license to say and do totally off-the-wall things they would never do at home. On top of that, our management just makes it worse. I don't get any sense of what the hotel stands for except selling rooms, and what's worse is that they don't seem to care if I stay or not."

"Oh, I'm sorry, Ari. Let me make my phone call, and then let's talk more about that. I think it is so unfortunate when people are unhappy at work, especially when I love my job so much. I feel kind of selfish, to tell you the truth."

"Well, that's the way of the world these days. Why don't you make your phone call, and then I'll make mine?"

———

Cora extracted the phone from her handbag and called her Jersey relatives to tell them she would be late. She was a bit annoyed that they weren't surprised; they even told her they never expected her to be on time anyway. Somehow, the daylight saving time excuse didn't seem to help.

"That *was* short and sweet," Ari said. "Thanks. Didn't sound like they were upset."

"I have this 'unfortunate reputation,' someone once called it, of being 'unfortunately tardy.' I simply *can't* explain it properly," Cora said through clenched teeth, mocking an upper-crust Connecticut Yankee accent that she had heard countless times in the hotel.

"Don't sweat it," Ari responded. "They'll be happy to see you, and all will be forgiven."

Time Management Practices
1. Prioritize tasks based on daily levels of urgency.
2. Gain closure on tasks by completing them as soon as possible.
3. Ensure meetings are concise and planned, and help to achieve objectives.
4. Seek a balance among work, family, and friends.
5. Manage free time to include hobbies, relaxation, reading, and exercise.

"You're right, but I don't like people thinking I am always playing catch-up. That's not something to cultivate. And I hate starting off every conversation with an apology about being late. But back to you. You were talking about your situation at work. Tell me more."

Ari exhaled loudly. "Oh, I don't want to complain. Nobody likes to hear these things. Everybody in corporate America is unhappy at work. My story is nothing unusual. You're the rarity—somebody who actually *likes* her job."

"You know, Ari, I have always felt people have to work hard not to become comfortable in their own misery because that misery often rubs off on other people. Why can't you change jobs? There must be hundreds of places that would appreciate someone with your skills—especially in New York City. You don't want to turn fifty and look back and say, 'If only I had changed jobs when I was thirty,' do you?"

Ari was taken aback for longer than he expected. Who *was* this woman, anyway? He felt she was exactly the tonic he needed.

"How'd you get so smart?" he asked. "Are you one of those undercover human resources people?"

"Not at all. I just think that people can either embrace their jobs and create a better life for themselves, or have a horrible time at work and probably an even worse time at home. They usually go hand in hand, you know. The one thing we can all manage is our attitude. Is the glass half-empty or half-full? It makes a big difference on our outlook on life and how we affect other people—especially our guests and their experiences at the hotel."

Their free-flowing conversation was interrupted by the chirp of Ari's cell phone.

"Let me see who this is, and we'll get back to that point in a minute."

He looked at the caller ID, even though he could have easily predicted the caller. It was his colleague and best-friend-at-work Anne Livingston. She was probably having a very lonely Sunday reading the *New York Times* aloud to Oscar, her crazy pet parrot.

"I'm on the train and talking to a really interesting woman," Ari said into the phone, turning and smiling at Cora. "Can we make this short, sweetie?"

"A woman, Ari?" she asked with some curiosity in her voice. "Sure, but I thought you should know about the e-mail I just got from our boss. Evil lurks in your in-box. You know the E-Mail Maniac usually waits for Sunday to deliver the *really* bad news. Do you want a preview or not?"

"Well, duh! Of course I do. What is it this time?"

Managing by E-mail

1. Remember that people will be reading your message at various times of day and in various stages of professional engagement.
2. Make sure to delete any portions of an e-mail thread that some employees should not see.
3. Reread the message for clarity and tone twice, if not three, times before pressing Send.
4. Restrict copies to people who really have a need-to-know.
5. E-mail is not the best vehicle for delivering bad news. Always meet with impacted employees face-to-face.

Cora listened while trying to be discreet about it.

"He's now saying one of the online travel sites has decided to delist the hotel because of all the negative comments people have been making. Do you realize what that means? We'll be getting an even *lower* class of customer."

"Oh my God, Annie. It's bad enough already. That's horrible news."

"I know, I know. And I suspect it will mean we might have to cut our rates and maybe even lay off some staff."

"Let's not go there just yet. But I realize the implications." Ari looked at Cora and grimaced.

"You'd better be prepared for a nasty week at work, Ari," Anne said. "This looks and sounds really serious."

"You know, doll, I just can't think about all this right now. It's Sunday, and I had been looking forward to a stress-free train ride. I even bought a sexy new novel to read. I don't need this additional agita in my life today. Let's talk when I get back, okay?"

Ari closed his phone and turned immediately to Cora. "Want to switch jobs?"

———

Almost as if on cue, the train came to an abrupt halt, causing passengers headed back from the café car to lurch, spilling several sodas and beers in the process.

"Ladies and gentlemen, we are temporarily delayed because of an electrical problem at the Baltimore station," the conductor announced. "We expect to be moving shortly."

"Here we go," Cora said. "I don't need to have my cousins think I am going to be even later."

"Oh, it happens all the time on this train," Ari said. "It shouldn't take long. Is this your first time riding the Acela? They *claim* it's the fastest way around the Eastern Corridor, but if you were in such a hurry, maybe you should have flown."

"No, I prefer the train, but it has been awhile since I've taken this one," she said. "I work in the hospitality business, so I should be more patient with these kinds of things. It's just I already feel bad enough having them think I am constantly late."

"Oh, don't worry about it. That's why cell phones were invented. I spend a fortune every month so my friends can call me to either ask directions or tell me they're going to be late. Those are the joys of telecom."

"Gosh, Ari, you sound just a little bit cynical," she said, carefully choosing her words. "Is that what living in New York does?"

He smiled, not at all offended.

"I *am* cynical, and that's why it wouldn't be so easy to get another job. People have actually called me a misanthrope—to my face! But it's not just New York. It's the cost of living in New York, the millions of people in New York, the awful, low-paying jobs you are forced to take to have a decent apartment in New York. It's all that."

The train resumed its journey, and Cora's mood brightened.

"Whew! I thought we might be stuck for a while. We have some of those same problems in San Francisco, but people just don't seem to take them so seriously out there. Maybe it's the weather."

"It's not the weather. I think they're all stoned!"

Cora blanched noticeably.

"I'm kidding, I'm kidding," Ari said hurriedly. "I think that people are just more tightly wound in Manhattan, being on that little island with millions of people who often don't even speak the same language. I swear, if I didn't speak Spanish, French, and Hebrew, I would probably be even more cynical. The bad part about speaking several languages is that sometimes you hear people saying things about you when they think you don't understand!"

"You are so right," Cora responded. "In fact, I am always amazed when some of our staff are talking among themselves thinking that no one else can hear them, but in fact, others are within earshot of the comments—even guests."

Cora took another gulp of water. The train was quite hot.

"Catch this story," Ari said. "Last summer I was in an elevator with my good friend Elizabeth. Her family is from Puerto Rico, so she speaks Spanish very well and we speak it together so I can practice. A woman wearing a horrible straw hat—a boater I guess you'd call it—got in the elevator with us. Elizabeth turned to me and said under her breath, 'Es como un panqueque de mierda,' and since you speak Spanish, I'm sure you know what that means. As the woman was getting off the elevator, she said, with a beautiful Castilian accent, 'Con permiso, por favor.' She obviously understood her hat being called a 'crap pancake.' I have never been so embarrassed."

"Oh Dios mio!" Cora said, "That's awful. I've had some similar experiences because people don't know that I speak Spanish too. We have to look at the humor in them, don't you think? That's a funny story, but weren't we talking about how things are with your job? That phone call didn't sound encouraging. What was the bad news?"

He hesitated before responding, not knowing how much to go into with this stranger on a train. He took a deep breath and began.

"Being in the business, you know how important it is to have the online booking services on your side. My friend Anne, who works the desk with me most days, said one of the major ones was going to delist us because of the bad comments people who have stayed in our hotel have posted. You can't ever censor those, which is why so many people trust them."

"Ouch, Ari! I can't believe someone as nice as you would work in a fleabag hotel. But you know there are ways to respond to those comments that no hotel wants."

The term "fleabag" seemed to affect him viscerally.

"It's *not* a fleabag, Cora. It's actually a decent hotel. It's not the Ritz-Carlton or Four Seasons, but it certainly is acceptable for most tourists around the world. Not everyone needs all the amenities they probably would find at *your* hotel."

Cora noticed that a bit of industry competitiveness had entered into the conversation. She remembered an article she had recently read about the new world of customers who relied exclusively on comments from the online booking sites before making reservations.

"Hey, I'm sorry if I offended you, my friend. My hotel is certainly not the Ritz-Carlton or the Four Seasons or the W, but people care about being comfortable and being treated nicely and made to feel you are glad to see them back again. It's all about making people feel a part of the family. It's like that in any business. Take good care of people once, and they will not only come back again but also tell their friends about you. We try to do our best to make everyone feel 'a part of,' rather than 'apart from,' and that includes both team members *and* guests."

She reached for her bag and notebook again.

"I'm going to write down the name of the online site that had some real strategies for dealing with negative customer comments about their experiences in hotels around the world. Everybody has to deal with them from time to time."

Ari chuckled to himself. His manager had lectured the entire staff about this new phenomenon, saying mainly that it was dominated by malcontents who would never be happy. He felt it was already too late for his own hotel's future, but was happy to hear about another's experience with the new world of Internet booking.

The train halted abruptly again, this time even more dangerously. The luggage above shifted noticeably. Fellow passengers looked at each other nervously.

"I don't know about you," Cora said, "but I am worried. It's not even bad weather, and we are dealing with these kinds of delays. How do you manage all these problems in the East?"

"Honey, this is nothing. When you've dealt with terrorist attacks, blackouts, and killer snowstorms, you learn to live on the edge. You seem quite the sophisticate. I can't believe you're so skittish. We'll get there—believe me!"

Cora suddenly realized she had not had time to eat anything before leaving her hotel for Union Station. She opened her purse and found a Kasha bar she always put aside for emergencies.

"I *do* believe you, but I am very concerned about being even later than I thought I might be. My cousins always tease me about it."

"Why are you so worried about your family?" Ari asked. "You seem so sure of yourself, yet you continue to talk about how they perceive you. It doesn't make sense. These things happen all the time. It's our souped-up world. Why are you so hard on yourself?"

The audio system crackled again.

"Ladies and gentlemen, we are still experiencing electrical problems at the Baltimore station," the conductor announced. "We should be moving shortly."

"You're right," Cora responded, munching the healthy snack. "I shouldn't be so concerned about what people think, but they trained us at the hotel to be totally professional and I don't think being constantly late is professional at all. Sorry to talk with my mouth full, but I haven't had a thing to eat today."

"I had something at the station, but I am dying to get a beer and a hot dog or two from the café car. It's something I always do when I take the train, just like when I'm at Yankee Stadium."

"So does that mean you're a baseball fan, Ari? That's one game I just cannot figure out."

"Yes, I am a huge baseball fan, and the world is full of baseball metaphors that I can 'get' because of it. Management books constantly refer to 'the rules of the game,' 'who's on first,' 'hitting a home run,' and stuff like that. The workplace is very much like the baseball diamond, but most of us don't get those big salaries."

Cora didn't like where this was headed. She was enjoying chatting with this appealing young guy, but she knew she was "out of her league," so to speak, if they were going to be discussing baseball.

"I don't even want to go there," she said. "I'm sure you can make your point well. I'm really more concerned about you not being happy in your job. What do you think you can do about that?"

"This is the kind of thing I usually talk about in therapy, so I'll buy you a hot dog instead of paying your fee." He laughed and stopped to reflect, just as the train resumed its very slow trek to New York.

"I really am happy that you like, make that *love*, your job, Cora, but mine is miserable. All the good things I originally thought I would like about it have turned to crap! People are jerks and have enormous expectations that I don't think anybody could meet, and management is even worse. They constantly promise things they don't deliver, and they treat us all like we should be down on our knees thanking them for giving us this great opportunity. I swear, there is going to be a worker revolt one of these days."

"Well, that could very well happen. But have you examined your own role in how these things have played out? Sometimes we inadvertently play into their hands."

Ari's eyebrows arched toward the overheads. He suddenly thought this woman might be one of "the enemy."

"What do you mean?"

Cora realized immediately she had touched a nerve.

"Well, all our team members like to see what they can do to create the 'extras' for the guest. It's about going above and beyond in providing service, with the goal of achieving extraordinary guest satisfaction. We call it 'customer delight.' It's a part of our core values and goes along with the hotel's vision and mission statement." Cora could see the pupils of Ari's eyes enlarge.

"Okay, cynical Ari is listening. Tell me more about this stuff," he requested, reluctantly.

"Well," said Cora, "it is all about creating what we call service culture tools, which enable team members all to be on the same page and going in the same direction. Our vision statement is simply *'To become the finest boutique hotel in San Francisco,'* and our mission statement tells us how we are going to do that. We developed these ourselves in a series of meetings, along with our guiding management principles and service standards. We even have a motto: *'We do it right, or we make it right.'*

"All these tools fit together and really help us make the difference in whether people make reservations with us or not, whether people will return on their next trip or not, and whether people will recommend us to their friends or not. Have I bored you to death yet?"

Who Are Our Guests?

1. Guests are the most important people in the world of hospitality.

2. Guests are not dependent on us—we are dependent on them.

3. Guests are not an interruption to our business—they are the purpose for our business.

4. Guests are not someone with whom to match wits. No one has ever won an argument with a guest.

5. Guests are people who bring us their NEWS—*n*eeds, *e*xpectations, *w*ants, and *s*uggestions—so that we may be of even greater service.

6. It is our responsibility to provide each guest with our finest products, services, and experiences.

"Wow," Ari said coldly, "I guess my hotel hasn't evolved as far as yours. I feel like I have met the enemy and it is us. I am going to go get a beer. How about that hot dog?"

"Ari, Ari, I am not trying to cause friction, but sometimes I think we need to question how we respond to the things that happen to us. You seem perfectly reasonable, but we were taught at my hotel that there are always several outcomes that can happen in any given situation. If you imagine that the worst will happen, it usually does."

He sat down again, heavily.

"You're right, but it hurts to hear that when you're going through it every day. I want to stay in touch with you. I think you could be a good influence in my life. Can we exchange e-mail addresses?"

"I'd really like that," she answered. Cora rifled through her handbag looking for that always-elusive pen at the bottom.

"I don't want you to think my situation is perfect, by any means," she said, "but maybe we can learn from one another. I certainly am willing to share what I know with you, and I will send you information on our program called Total Peak Performance. I truly believe that it's through sharing best practices that everyone benefits in raising the service bar. Also, I believe in fate—that there's a reason people meet each other. We've got another couple of hours, you know, but let's talk about more interesting topics— like your exciting life in New York City. I'll bet it's fascinating. Now please go for *your* beer and *my* hot dog."

Questions for Group Discussion

1. Cora talks repeatedly about lateness not being considered professional. Are there people in your organization who deal with this issue? Is it because they are not organized or because of the pace of the world at large? What are some suggestions for better time management?

2. At Cora's hotel, management stresses the importance of addressing guests by name. Do you think that could make a difference in customer loyalty at your own workplace? Under what circumstances could you use the guest's or customer's name more often?

3. Ari admits to being "cynical." In your experience, is that a bad or a good description of a person's character? Some would argue that cynical people are simply more realistic, particularly considering the state of corporations and the service industry as a whole. Do you agree?

4. Cora tells Ari that there are many outcomes for any situation. Do you agree? What role does your own attitude play in those various outcomes?

5. Ari believes Cora is "the rarity—somebody who actually *likes* her job." What percentage of people do you think:

    _____ are passionate about their job?

    _____ love their job?

    _____ like their job?

    _____ dislike their job?

    _____ hate their job?

    100%

6. E-mail mania is prevalent throughout businesses today. Some people depend on it almost exclusively for communication. What are some of the shortcomings of overusing or abusing e-mail?

7. Fellow employees and guests often can overhear comments not intended for them. This can cause hurt feelings at the very least. Share some awkward situations you have experienced or heard about. What can be done to correct them?

8. Cora mentions vision, mission, core values, guiding management principles, service standards, and systems as tools necessary for team members to all be on the same page. What tools do you have? How do they work? What needs to be done to have them be even more effective?

9. The one thing we can all manage is our attitude. Is the glass half-empty or half-full? Discuss how changing one's attitude can often change the outcome of a difficult situation.

Chapter 2

For Better or for Worse

Not everything that is faced can be changed, but
nothing can be changed until it is faced.
—James Baldwin

Cora made a point of setting the alarm a half hour earlier than usual on her first day back at work at the Hotel Metronome in San Francisco. The visit to her relatives' home in New Jersey was pleasant enough, but she had often bristled hearing repeated references to her problems with punctuality. Her cousins practiced curtsying while referring to her as "Your Chronic Lateness," instead of "Your Royal Highness." She was not amused.

Getting the twins' breakfasts ready always took longer than she planned, and she hated feeling rushed making her way into work. She and her husband, Jason, had talked calmly on the way back from the airport about sharing the parenting duties a bit more, particularly as the twins were getting older. There was bound to be more chauffeuring duties than before, and she told him there should be a term for dads as much in use as "soccer mom."

Cora reflected several times during the visit to her cousins about the conversation she and Ari had on the train. She often told people how grateful she was that she enjoyed her job so much, and realized that the statement was usually met with derision and disbelief. How had the workplace become so toxic for so many people? With all the management books out there (and her husband read many of them), how had management failed the worker so badly? She realized these were rhetorical questions, but she made a pledge that if she were ever in a position of real authority, she would do her part to make things better. That probably wasn't possible just yet in her desk clerk job. Or was it?

———

"Well, well, look who's back," the hotel's general manager Will Jameson called after her as Cora made her way through the Art Deco lounge. The hotel's signature collection of metronomes ticked away as usual. "We missed you, and so did a lot of the guests. Did you have a good time? How was Washington?"

"Hey, Will," Cora said, as if to an old friend, "I missed you all, too. I had a great time and learned a lot. Thanks for letting me go. I know it created a bit of a stretch for the rest of the staff. I brought back little presents for everybody, but how many miniature Washington Monuments does the world need, anyway? Seriously, I really did miss you, but the weather was perfect and my trip to New Jersey was fun as well. I hadn't seen my cousins in a long time. They gave me the same kidding about being late that you do, so I've decided to make a real effort to be better about that."

Her boss looked genuinely surprised.

"Cora, we love you and think you do a fantastic job. I can live with you being ten minutes late on occasion, but I hate seeing you so stressed right after you've arrived. I think that's a good self-realization, but believe me, that's the least of my challenges running this place. Now, let's get to work!"

Cora hurried the hundred feet or so to her position behind the reception desk. Her good friend Caitlin Gold was almost finished balancing receipts from the early departures. Bellman and party-boy Damien Townsend was helping an elderly couple get their belongings out to the van waiting to take them on a tour of Napa Valley and its justly famous vineyards.

"Hey, doll!" Caitlin said, throwing her arms around Cora. She was genuinely happy to have her back. "I am so glad to see you. I thought about you every day since you've been gone. Gosh, we missed you. How was it?"

"Oh, sweetie, it was terrific. I met so many interesting people and got some great ideas about how we might be able to change things for the better around here."

"Oh my God," Caitlin said, rolling her eyes. "Here we go. Changing things for the better usually means disaster. Things are just fine around here. You know that."

"Well, you know there really isn't any *status quo* anymore. Either we are constantly getting better as we provide our guest experiences or we are getting worse. There is no in-between. Nothing is stationary, so 'That's good enough' never should be. We all need to look at what, how, and why we are doing things in the light of continuous improvement. Everyone needs to put on the hat of being a quality engineer. If changes are needed, they have to be communicated upward for action and follow-up."

"Somebody's been to hotel school," Caitlin said derisively but with genuine affection. "You'll be running the place soon. And then I'll have to kill you."

Cora realized she was sounding a bit too much like a tool of management. She thought for a moment and remembered the handout of the "Ten Commandments of Running a Great Business" they had given out at the convention. Amazingly, she thought, it could be used in any business setting. She knew it was in her backpack in the staff lounge.

"I have something that we should all take a look at around here. Let me get it."

Cora rushed to the back of the hotel and returned out of breath. She was determined not to lose this chance to make her point.

"Here," she said, handing the single sheet of paper to her coworker with some bravura. "This was one of my biggest takeaways from the hotel convention."

Caitlin carefully read it with early disdain that gradually turned into grudging acceptance. "You know what? This is absolutely right on. You should show it to Will and make sure he posts it. We all need reinforcement on these points from time to time."

The Ten Commandments of Business Success
1. Commit to company vision and mission.
2. Embrace company core values.
3. Provide employees with needed resources.
4. Follow service standards to ensure levels of performance and consistency.
5. Engage in meaningful relationships.
6. Be as transparent as you can in all business dealings.
7. Strive to exceed customer expectations.
8. Support a climate of open and clear communication.
9. Be passionate in everything you do.
10. Develop pride in self, company, and your job.

Damien sauntered back toward the reception area. Both women enjoyed his edgy personality, but they had heard the more reserved

British guests refer to him as "cheeky." He worked hard and played even harder, and had easily as many admirers as detractors. It didn't hurt that he was Hollywood handsome.

"So, Corazon," he said teasingly, using Cora's given name, "did you get into any trouble back East? Anything you want to tell me? A beautiful single woman in the big city? No kids to worry about? I am living my life vicariously these days, so tell all."

Cora was accustomed to seeing Damien in action, so she knew it was just his way of being flirtatious.

"Not single—just traveling singly. And vicariously—you? No way. You're the party animal of all time. How many times were you out 'sick' while I was gone?"

"Only once," Caitlin answered quickly. "And I think it might have even been legitimate for once."

"That's right, dude. I've decided to clean up my act. I'm getting older, and I want to settle down. But you didn't answer my question, Cora. Were your wicked ways working?"

"You are too much! I was one of the vestal virgins, as usual. Besides, I had a lot going on. I was there on business, you may recall. But by the way, I have decided to make a big change, too. I have decided to work on my 'lateness problem.'"

Both Caitlin and Damien seemed taken aback—and a little nostalgic. They had enjoyed hours of teasing Cora because of her vulnerability in the time-management area.

"I'll believe it when I see it," Damien said offhandedly, hurrying to aid another couple off for a day of sightseeing.

"Don't mind him, Cora," Caitlin said. "It's probably your only flaw, and it's a minor one at that. Nobody here minds covering for you for a few extra minutes. After all, that's part of teamwork. Much better than Damien calling in sick when he has a hangover, which he does all the time. He's on the verge of getting the axe, I think. I overheard Will talking to a guest who was complaining that Damien was 'too familiar' and Will saying he would speak to him. If he's really 'cleaning up his act,' I'll bet it's because Will is on his case. And you *know* that Will can do just that, despite how nice he seems on the outside."

Damien walked into the reception area from the side door just in time to hear the last part of Caitlin's statement.

"Are you two talking about me? If you are, tell me to my face. I hate being gossiped about—unless it's in the pages of *Vanity Fair*."

"Cait was just giving me an update on what's been going on around here," Cora said. "Sounds like things are about normal. Tell me more about the New You, anyway. Cleaning up your act? Settling down? Seems a little far-fetched to me. What brought this on?"

"Well, Cait was right," Damien said, looking a little sheepish. "I got a call to 'the office.' Will told me people have said that I had been a little familiar to them, especially when the elevator was out last week and I had to haul more bags up and down the stairs than usual. I was just trying to make light of a difficult situation, that's all. Geez, people are so touchy these days."

"You know, Damien, not everyone has the same sense of humor as you do," Cora replied. "At the hotel I was staying at last week in Washington, I sat down in the lobby for extended periods and just observed how the desk clerks responded to various guests. It was easily as instructional as attending the convention itself. One afternoon a man with a thick German accent checked in, and the desk clerk, an attractive black woman with a little bit of an attitude, was trying to be funny and charming with him, telling him about the hotel's amenities and a bit about the immediate neighborhood. He, however, thought she was being flippant and was having none of it.

"I was worried," Cora continued. "I thought it might have turned really ugly. Almost immediately, the desk clerk sensed that the guest had just gotten off a long flight and was tired, and probably not in the best of moods. She turned on a dime and very seriously said, 'You just want to go to bed, don't you? Here's your passkey. Room 612. Enjoy your stay and don't hesitate to call if you need anything at all. The elevators are just around the corner, across from the gift shop.' Sometimes you have to read a guest in just a few seconds. That's the big secret of working in the service industries."

"That's a nice story, Cora," Damien said. "I'll try and remember it. I just wish people would tell me to my face rather than ratting me out to my boss."

"Damien, it's up to *you* to read a guest's body language and demeanor. Particularly for the more reserved types, your style—which most people find funny and very personal—could rub them the wrong way. You have to be able to be there for each person and adapt to that customer. That's all I'm saying."

"Give me an example, Little Miss Hospitality."

"Well, first you have to be completely present and in the moment with each person you encounter. Pay attention and listen carefully to the message that the customer's communicating. Read between the lines to what the person is saying and *not* saying, and lastly, know when to move from your own world into theirs. Over and out."

———

The two early shifters went home for the day, leaving Cora alone for ten minutes until her "partner in crime," the amusing but sometimes vicious Tim Olmos arrived—late as usual. He, like Cora, had a problem setting alarm clocks.

"Oh my God," Tim said, out of breath. "That hill gets steeper every day. If this city were flat, I would have no problem getting here on time. Give me a kiss, sweetie pie. How was Washington? Did your hick cousins get you into Manhattan at least once?"

"Washington was mostly work, and unfortunately I never made it into Manhattan this time. My cousins have become discount outlet junkies, and they don't have any in the city. But I met this really nice guy on the train from Washington who lives there and who also works in a hotel. I almost feel like I got into the city because we really hit it off, and he told me a lot about living there. I suspect we'll become friends. He e-mailed me last week, and I owe him a response. He was terrific, but it sounds like he's got a bad situation at work. Anyway, what's been going on? Tell me everything."

"Well, sugar, things aren't so great around here, if you ask me," Tim said too readily. "Damien is probably not going to make it, and Ella is on our backs up here. Lucy, the head of housekeeping, left last week, and they can't find anybody who can speak the languages she did. You know how critical that is when you're working with people from all over the world. I don't think they did a thing to keep her."

"Lucy left?" Cora asked incredulously. "Now *that* is terrible news. I liked her so much, too."

"And get ready for this," Tim said wickedly. "They sent the new bartender to rehab because she was 'sampling' a little too much during the free wine pourings every night. One of the guests told me when he was checking out that he saw her giving her number to three different guys."

Cora laughed. She had missed a lot in just a couple of weeks.

"You mean what's-her-name? That really 'beautiful but don't touch me' chick? She's in rehab? I thought she was only part-time."

"That's true, but Ella felt sorry for her and pleaded to Will for the hotel to pay for it. You didn't hear this from me, by the way. It's all thirdhand."

"Well, with you it always is, no?" Cora asked. "What's up with Ella? Why is she coming down so hard on us?"

"Oh, you mean Cruella? She's the same. We rarely see her. She stays down in the kitchen most of the time. She seems to like managing the restaurant, though, so they get to see plenty of her— poor fools. The guests love her, of course. They don't see the extra work we all have to do because she's so desperate to be liked that she volunteers us to do things for them all the time. She wants us to be known as the Nordstrom's of the hotel world. I absolutely draw the line at going out and changing a guest's flat tire."

"You?" Cora asked. "I doubt you would know where to put the jack. I remember one time she asked me to go home and get the twins' stroller because one of the guests had lost theirs through careless baggage handling. I reminded her mine was for twins, and she said, 'They can put the diaper bag in the extra seat.' It took nearly an hour round-trip, but guess who got all the nice kudos on TripAdvisor.com? Ella is the name. But, hey, it's about teamwork, right?"

"Oh, absolutely, but catch this," Tim said. "Last week a small advertising firm from Sausalito was having a retreat in the conference room overlooking the garden. They asked if we had a DVD player they could use to show some new commercials they had made to a potential client. Rather than telling them no, she offered to go and buy one and bill them for it later. Well, guess who had to go get it? That would be me."

"You know, Tim, I'm sorry about that. But we really *should* have a DVD player available if they want to encourage meetings here. I realize from that convention in Washington that there are a number of things we should change around here. You know I love this place, but it's not perfect. Our phone system totally sucks. How many complaints do you get about it every day? If Russell Crowe ever stays here, I am going to have to quit!"

"Well, you're right about that, and about the timing, too, I think. I don't mind change if it's done thoughtfully, and Will was just saying the other day that the parent company had plans for upgrading this hotel. It has the highest occupancy rate in the whole chain. People like this place, despite its faults."

"Oh, that's really good news, Tim. Customers always expect a top-notch experience, and I'm so glad to hear the corporate office is considering some renovations. Also, sometimes a quality experience doesn't necessarily mean providing more. Sometimes it's just providing something different and unique from the competition. It's that outside-the-box thinking that can make the difference in our products, services, and the hotel experience itself."

Make Someone's Day
1. Create memorable events that make a positive difference for others.
2. Choose to take the extra step you didn't have to take.
3. Focus on giving, not getting.
4. Become a customer-interaction engineer by putting people together.
5. Always treat customer feedback as a gift.

Will Jameson, who had been a few feet away in the lobby reading the *Wall Street Journal,* heard all that the two had said. He decided to file most of the information for future use but to speak to the last remark immediately.

"That's true, you guys. And you both play an enormous role in this hotel's success. Never forget that. I'm convinced that it's our team members who create the fantastic customer loyalty this hotel enjoys. My job is to make sure the powers that be in our corporate office never forget that, nor the two of you. And I want you to know that in terms of serving the public, you two have raised the bar pretty high.

"When you see a familiar face or repeat guest in the lobby," he continued, "you always make the additional effort to spend a few minutes with them. You ask about their stay, see if there is anything further they need, find out about their travel schedules and when they plan to return to the city so you might book an advance reservation. In short, you are all about connecting with the guest and making their day. And you make *my* day by doing just that."

Questions for Group Discussion

1. Cora reflects that the workplace has become toxic for many people. Do you agree? What can management do to ensure employees feel honored and empowered in a "souped-up world."

2. While most people say that change is inevitable, Caitlin doubts that changing things "for the better" can be accomplished easily. Why do you think she feels that way? Have you gone through change initiatives that have been difficult? Is there anything you could have done to make that process easier?

3. Will called Damien to his office and talked to him about "guest familiarity." What one guest sees as overly familiar another may view as just friendly, but perception for each individual is his or her reality. Comment on your experiences with guests and employees regarding differing perceptions of the same situations.

4. Cora says that the big secret of working in the service industry is being able to "read" a customer in just a few seconds. Have you experienced a customer interaction that might have turned ugly if it hadn't been defused by a well-trained employee?

5. There is quite a lot of information exchanged after Cora returns from her two-week trip. Is it gossip, or simply bringing Cora up-to-date? Can gossip ever be a positive force in the workplace? Explain.

6. Ella is not seen in a favorable light primarily because of her belief in the customer always being right. Can a customer ever be too demanding? How would you deal with a customer who you felt could never be pleased completely?

7. In recent weeks, Damien has become overly familiar with guests beyond the bounds of the "just friendly" standards of the job. If you were his manager, how would you handle the situation? Where would you talk to him? When?

8. Quality experiences do not always mean providing more, but rather something different and unique from the competition. How do you differentiate your products, services, and the hotel experience itself from the competition?

9. Will talks about how employees can become sales agents as part of their job. How can team members who come in contact with customers become more active sales agents? Thinking about this from a sales and marketing perspective, what are the special features and customer benefits of your organization?

Chapter 3

Coping with Crisis

Coming together is a beginning. Keeping together
is progress. Working together is success.
—Henry Ford

Ari Libman loved documentary films almost as much as
he loved politics. He spent much of his life, his colleague
Anne Livingston often reminded him, at the Film Forum in lower
Manhattan, which specialized in showing nonmainstream fare.
He recently saw a new documentary about the 1988 presidential
campaign, when Michael Dukakis lost to George H. W. Bush.
In the vice-presidential debate, much-maligned Dan Quayle
attempted to equate himself with the much-loved John F. Kennedy.
His opponent, Lloyd Bentsen, the esteemed Texas senator who had
been in the military with JFK, quipped famously, "Mr. Quayle, I
served with Jack Kennedy. I was a friend of Jack Kennedy. And you,
sir, are no Jack Kennedy."

Ari's Hotel Metro was no Hotel Metronome. Located exactly
midway between Times Square and Macy's, the hotel benefited

from travel books that remarked upon its proximity to those two major Big Apple destinations—and its "value for the dollar." Foreigners planning on both shopping and theatergoing often thought they couldn't find a better situation. And right off Fifth Avenue, too? What a bonus!

Ari had enjoyed the train conversation with Cora as well and e-mailed her almost as soon as he returned to the city. He thought she might be able to help him see his career situation in a somewhat more generous light. He hadn't yet heard back from her, but he knew she was with her relatives for a week.

His own week could not have been worse. The delisting of the hotel from the travel website had an immediate impact. Online booking dropped precipitously, meaning that the marketing and PR department would have to rely on courting the various travel publications that had high readerships abroad. But his general manager waited the entire next week before calling an all-hands meeting for Monday morning to address the situation. *Typical,* Ari thought.

"Folks, we are in crisis mode," his boss, Dale Rothman, proclaimed. "We are going to have to hunker down. We don't want to have to lay anybody off, even though times are very challenging right now."

The mood in the meeting was poisonous. Ari's colleagues started whispering among themselves just as Dale started speaking again.

"This is a war situation. If our Internet bookings fall off dramatically, we are probably not going to make it. I am going to rely on each of you to go the extra mile to make sure the guests we *do* have are comfortable and happy and tell every single person they can about the hotel. You are going to be on the front lines. *You* are going to have to remind them to talk us up, wherever they happen to be from."

Ari was not buying it. A good hotel would have never allowed this to happen in the first place. A good hotel would have never allowed things to disintegrate to this level. A *good* hotel would have spent the money to not just hire the best people but also to train and empower them properly. Sadly, Ari realized, he didn't work for a good hotel.

Handling Customer Complaints
1. Recognize the guest immediately.
2. Be completely focused on what the guest is saying.
3. Refrain from interrupting the guest.
4. Use the principles of active listening to make sure you understand completely what the guest has told you.
5. Apologize on behalf of the company.
6. Explain what you are going to do to resolve the situation.
7. Thank the guest for bringing the "problem" to your attention.
8. Follow up to make sure the problem has been taken care of.

As they all were dismissed after another dressing-down, Ari decided to call Cora, his San Francisco train buddy. Maybe she, not knowing all the details of the situation, might offer a shoulder worth crying on. Maybe she, happy as the proverbial clam in her work situation, could be helpful in understanding just how difficult his work situation was and how much more difficult it might become.

The phone at the Metronome rang as the hotel staff started checking out their biggest roster of the day. Mondays were referred to as "turnover days" because almost every room got a new guest.

"Hi, Cora, is that you?" Ari asked. "This is your cynical hotel friend from New York. I didn't get a response to my e-mail last week, so I thought I would just pick up the phone and call you. I got the number from your website. I didn't know your hotel was part of a chain. We should probably look into that, too."

"Oh, Ari, hello. I was at my cousins' house last week and just got back last night. I haven't had time yet to respond to all the e-mails. The twins have been a little sick, so it has been hectic around the house. Plus at this moment, we are really busy in the hotel. Could I call you back when the rush is over?"

"Oh, I'm so sorry. I always forget that we're three hours ahead of you. It's probably checkout time in San Francisco. I'll call you in an hour or so."

Cora hung up as Damien returned from hailing yet another taxi for a departing guest.

"Guess who's coming in today?" Cora asked. "One of your favorites."

"Really? Who?"

"The British guy, Mr. Wade," she answered. "You know, the one with the bow ties."

Damien had to think a minute; many of their British guests wore bow ties.

"Oh, him, yeah. He's a great tipper."

"It's not about that, Damien," Cora chastised. "He's a great guy overall. I think he's been here thirty-something times. That's why this hotel has the highest occupancy rate in the chain. People not only come back—they tell their friends. He told me once his business partner recommended this place years ago, and he's been staying here ever since."

Another guest, looking a little bleary-eyed, exited from the overtaxed elevator to settle her bill. Cora suspected it had not been an easy night for her.

"Room 311," the woman said. "Checking out."

Cora pulled up the guest's charges on her terminal. "I hope you enjoyed your stay with us, Ms. Seschil?" Cora said uncertainly. "Sorry ... how is that pronounced?"

"Cecil, like the man's name. The middle 'S' is silent. It's an old Danish name."

"Got it. Sorry. Was everything to your satisfaction, Ms. Seschil? The room was billed to your company, but they didn't cover your incidental expenses. Did you have anything from the minibar last night?"

The Danish woman nodded.

"And what would that have been?"

"The minibar," she said, blushing.

"Excuse me, but what exactly from the minibar did you have?" Cora asked, wondering if the woman's lack of fluency in English might be causing the miscommunication.

"I had the minibar. The *entire* minibar—except for the alcohol. I got in late last night from Seattle and hadn't had anything to eat. I didn't feel like going out again just for some juice and Coca-Colas. I am here on business, so I will put it on my expense account when I get back. My company *should* pay, since they sent me on this trip with only a day's notice."

Oh my, Cora thought. *This is going to cost something.* "I'll tell you what, Ms. Seschil, we'll comp the juice and sodas, but it's still going to be nearly fifty dollars on your bill," Cora informed the Danish visitor.

"That's really nice of you," she said. "It's so unusual to find staff who can make a decision these days."

Cora thought, *Thank goodness for those preshift meetings and discussions on how to handle delicate situations. Being empowered is a wonderful feeling.*

Empowering Employees, Part I

1. Allow employees to be the voice of management whenever possible.
2. Remind *every* employee that he or she is on the front lines with customers and guests.
3. Remember that the checkout procedure is the final memory a guest has of his or her experience. If a small sum is disputed, allow employees to make those determinations without involving management.
4. Praise employees who have resolved situations on their own.
5. When speaking of customer situations, focus only on the good.

The hour passed quickly with many guests checking out but still needing hand-holding on various fronts. Ari called again from New York just as one of the bellmen was retrieving the luggage for the last guest. Damien was occupied whistling for another cab.

"Oh, Ari, I am so glad to hear from you," Cora said, with genuine enthusiasm. "I have thought about you so often. How are things in New York?"

That was not the best question to ask. He launched into a typical Ari Libman tirade.

"I am trying to live by your words of wisdom, Cora, but it is just about impossible with people who lie to you and blame you for every little thing that happens. These awful people are going to get what they deserve. They have no ethics and no concern for our guests, but who gets to hear the complaints? We do! We make this big deal about not charging for parking, for instance, but when people take their cars out of the garage, there's a twenty-five-dollar charge. Of course they complain to us at the front desk, and we have to say, 'We don't charge to park, but we *do* charge to retrieve.' I mean, how deceptive is that? That was the subject of a lot of the complaints on that travel website that dropped us. We also got some comments about the front-desk staff being rude. But in my opinion, that's because we can't give guests what they want, like a free upgrade, so they think that *we're* the problem, not management."

Cora understood Ari's concern completely. She knew from years in the service industry that no customer likes surprises but that people generally appreciate the truth, even if it means paying extra. She also thought to herself, *It's not what you say to the guest but how you say it.*

"Oh, that's totally wrong, Ari. You have to work in a hotel like that? Well, it sounds to me like it's not going to make it in the long run. Why don't you talk to management about merging with or being bought by one of the smaller chains, like we did? It was my colleague Tim's idea, actually. The new owners are literally just down the street, and that totally keeps us on our toes because they drop in here all the time. It was our salvation, frankly. Then cash flow doesn't become such an issue, and improvements can be made over time."

"You know, that's something that maybe I *can* talk to my boss about. He seems so stressed out about cash all the time, and maybe that would be something he would consider. If we don't do something quickly, I think once word of mouth gets around, we are going to be finished. Can I ask you once again—how'd you get so smart?"

"Not smart, Ari, *savvy*. And I don't even live in New York."

Questions for Group Discussion

1. Ari's manager tells the employees that the company is in "crisis mode." Is that the best way to convey information? Do you think people want to know the whole truth, or would it be better to soften the message? Why?

2. Ari's hotel has had a series of difficulties that came on the heels of customers complaining online. How should management respond to customers who complain? How should employees on the front lines be trained to resolve customer complaints?

3. Cora tells Damien that the secret to the Metronome's success is people telling others about their experiences there. Have you heard that about your own company or service? Do you agree? What can employees do to ensure that guests and customers tell others?

4. Word of mouth has always been very powerful. Studies have shown that within seven days, a customer will tell ten others of a good experience but will tell fifty others of a negative one. Thanks to the Internet, customers can now influence millions of others. Comment on how this can impact your business.

5. Cora decided without consulting her boss to cover the cost of a portion of the guest's minibar bill. Do you think that was proper? Would you be allowed to make that determination without management's approval? Do you think it made a difference in the guest's experience?

6. People in general do not like surprises, particularly in an unfamiliar city. The Hotel Metro's parking policy alienates many guests. Could Ari have done something that would have made a difference? Do you think management listens to suggestions from both guests *and* employees? Share the experiences you have had with similar situations.

Chapter 4

A Spoonful of Sugar

Your most unhappy customers are your
greatest source of learning.
—Bill Gates

Cora and Tim were exchanging stories about some of the
recent guests ("Guess what!" Tim asked. "A guy in 520 had
two masseuses come in at the same time last Friday, and they
didn't like each other one bit!") when a taxi pulled up in front of
the hotel.

"Damien," Tim called, "there's a guest arriving who looks like
he might need some help."

A tall, dapper man with a yellow bow tie gathered two of the
bags himself, while leaving the remaining duffel on the sidewalk.
Damien arrived within seconds to collect it.

"Mr. Wade, let me have those," Damien said. "It's my job. I'll
get the trolley. You'll be happy to know that the elevator is working
this time."

"I suspect that you're happier about that than I am," Henry Wade joked. "That must be why you look heavier than the last time I was here."

"Ouch! That hurt. But I gave up smoking since then. That always puts on the pounds. Or the kilos, as you would say."

Both Cora and Tim grinned broadly as their British guest arrived at the front desk and took out his credit card case.

"Mr. Wade, so good to see you again. Welcome back to the Hotel Metronome," Tim said. "What brings you here this time?"

"I told you to call me Henry, and you never do, even though I call you Tim. It doesn't seem fair."

"That's just the way we're trained," Cora said. "We try and be as professional as we can here. And you actually *seem* like a Mr. Wade anyway."

"Well, call me what you want. I'm really glad to see you both— and you, too, Damien," he said as an afterthought. "I'm here for an entire week this time. I'll be supervising the printing of our annual report. It's so much less expensive here than in England. These days the dollar is so *advantageous*, shall we say, versus sterling."

Cora was surprised. "Is it? I didn't know that. But at least we'll get to see lots of you this time, right? When was the last time you were here?"

Henry Wade had to reflect for a moment before answering, "In January, right after the holidays. Remember how nice the climate was?"

"Yes, I do. People always talk about how upside-down our weather is," Tim said. "How many times do you think this makes for you here? Thirty or more?"

Cora had been busy at her computer terminal doing research on that very question.

"This is your thirty-sixth stay," she announced after counting the multitude of hotel folios in their database. "Can you believe it? Why do you keep coming back? I think I know, but I always like hearing it from the guests." *Tim needs to hear it more than I do,* she thought privately.

"If I have to stay in a hotel while I'm doing business, then I want it to feel as much like home as possible, and you do a wonderful job of anticipating my needs. I just feel that you really care about my comfort. Everything is always the way I expect it. I think that meeting expectations is one thing in the service world, but I think exceeding expectations is even more important. And consistency is just as vital. You deliver on all fronts."

Meeting Customers' NEWS (*n*eeds, *e*xpectations, *w*ants, *s*uggestions)

1. Ensure consistency in everything presented to the guest.
2. Be timely on delivering all services.
3. Take personal pride in "making everything happen" and "moving heaven and earth" for the guest.
4. Continuously seek out what steps you and others can take to improve performance.
5. Keep and update a personal notebook of key customers' NEWS.

"A chap I met on the plane coming here," Henry Wade continued, "told me he was returning to San Francisco after a few days in Bath, which you may know is a beautiful historic city right outside London. He had a terrible time in a luxurious hotel on the Crescent rather known for its pompous treatment of guests. He had a real series of mishaps, if you ask me. He said the only thing that worked in Bath was the bath itself! I asked him if he had complained to management, and he said no. I told him about this hotel and how I truly feel if I ever had reason to make a complaint, you would listen carefully and do whatever you could to correct it. Meanwhile, that fellow is probably going to tell his story to who knows how many people over the years? A negative report on a customer experience may be even more powerful than a glowing recommendation. I wish that managers would remember that."

"Mr. Wade," Cora said, "if you or any guest had a complaint, we certainly would listen with every intention of making it right. It's called having a 'recovery strategy.' In the service industry, every person should have his or her recovery strategies thought out ahead of time in the event something *does* go wrong. Even with the best of intents, sometimes it does. If I could control our heating or air-conditioning, or even the phone system, my life would be so much less stressed. But some things we just can't control. You realize that more than just about any of our guests. And we appreciate that."

Service Recovery Strategies
1. Treat defects, oversights, and mistakes as opportunities to learn.
2. Make it "more than right" the second time.
3. Take the HEAT—*h*ear them, *e*mpathize, *a*pologize, *t*ake action.
4. Follow up personally to make sure the situation has been corrected to the customer's satisfaction.
5. Remember: it costs nothing to recognize someone and a lot to ignore him or her.

"So right you are, Cora darling," he continued. "I don't know if you remember, but when I was here in January, I had to stay down the hill at your sister hotel. The Metronome was totally booked. The other hotel was perfectly fine, but completely impersonal compared to here. Actually, to tell you the truth, it was a little nicer than here on the surface, but I don't think one person on the staff ever even wished me, 'Good morning.' I remember queuing to check in for what seemed to be at least fifteen minutes, and no one even acknowledging me. It's the little things that count. Making eye contact, saying something to recognize that I am next, and hearing 'Good morning' are free!"

"That hotel is a recent acquisition," Will Jameson said as he poked his head out of the private office next to the front desk. "The staff there is still being trained in our parent company's ways, and I think it shows in the way they treat the guests. Thanks for being candid about it. I will pass your comments along to my boss. We don't often hear how we compare to the other hotels in the group, so your thoughts are appreciated. Now, let's check you in."

Make Customer Feedback Valuable

1. Have a plan to obtain feedback on a continuous and systematic basis.
2. Value all feedback as the breakfast of champions.
3. Remember: feedback presents opportunities to improve the service culture.
4. Establish an information forum to systematically discuss organizational challenges.
5. Pass on feedback to top management.

Ari decided a long swim was exactly what he needed after a brutal, stressful day at work. Everything Anne Livingston had predicted was already coming true. He had witnessed at least five instances of hostility toward both guests and coworkers in the days following the delisting. Should he listen to Cora's advice and start looking for another job? Or should he think about another profession entirely? Or what about merging with another hotel or chain?

He stopped at the Korean deli for some spinach and a hard-boiled egg for a healthy salad. His plan was to have a quiet evening at home and work on his resume. That plan went awry when his cell phone chirped. The caller ID told him it was Anne—as usual.

"Gosh, doll, we spend all day together, and you want to talk at night, too? Don't you get enough of me at work?"

"I could never get too much of you, Ari. I just wanted to hear a friendly voice, and this parrot can only offer so much. Besides, I wanted to talk seriously with you with nobody around to overhear us."

"Hey, I'm not quite home yet. I'll call you back in a few minutes on my landline, okay?"

He wanted to have a little time to make the salad. He could munch while Anne complained—he was certain that's what she wanted to do. He greeted the superintendent as he took the stairs two at a time to his third-floor apartment. It took him less than five minutes to prepare the salad and pour himself a glass of wine before dialing Anne's number.

"All right, sweetie," he said into the phone. "I want to be here for you. I am famished after my swim. I hope you don't mind if I eat while we chat. What's up anyway? What did you want to talk about?"

"Well, *work*, of course," she admitted. "What else do I ever talk about? What exactly are we going to do? I think it has gotten particularly bad these last few days. I think even the guests sense it, and that's why we have had such nasty scenes. Do you think we're going to be laid off? I heard the night accountant say something about not making payroll next time."

Choose Your Attitude

People can choose how they approach their day. The Disney Corporation says, "When in your role, everyone is 'on stage.' It is all smiles, greeting customers enthusiastically, and asking how you can be of assistance."

Exercise: Adopt a positive attitude to every situation, record how it makes a difference, and share your experience with other team members.

"Oh, that's just great, doll. My landlord will love that. While I was swimming at the Y tonight, I gave a lot of thought to getting a new job. I talked to the woman I met on the train last week. You know, the one who works in the hotel in San Francisco? She tries to be encouraging, but she doesn't know how bad things are here. She says, 'Try to be more upbeat.' 'Try to think of a good outcome.' 'Don't be so cynical.' Easier said than done, if you ask me."

Ari heard Oscar, the parrot, give his trademark wolf whistle in the background.

"She sounds like Mary Poppins to me," Anne said dismissively. "If she's got a good situation, then bully for her. But we are living this mess every day. Did you get a chance to say anything to our boss since the staff meeting?"

"No, I didn't see him at all. I'm sure he's purposefully avoiding us. I think I am going to talk to him about trying to partner with another hotel or maybe even urge him to think about being acquired by a small chain. Cora says that worked wonders for her hotel. They got a complete room renovation out of it. Also, their new reservation network that all the hotels share is helping to increase bookings."

"Well, that's an interesting concept, for sure, but you aren't his favorite 'ideas guy,' you know?" Anne said.

"I know, but if I can approach him with a solid proposal, then maybe he'll consider it. I should get off the phone, because I want to do a little Internet research on hotel acquisitions. About all I know is from playing *Monopoly*!"

Questions for Group Discussion

1. "It's my job," the bellman tells the hotel's British guest attempting to handle his own bags. Do you think most people have a fundamental understanding of what constitutes "their job"? Do you? Is just doing one's job enough these days? Why?

2. In successful guest service positions, the "job" is made up of 20 percent technical knowledge and 80 percent human relations. What is your job mix? How does this relate to your team? What role do you play in the bigger picture of the company's success?

3. Mr. Wade says the reason he's a repeat guest is because the hotel anticipates his needs well. What does that mean as to how you treat your own customers? How does the Golden Rule—Treat others as you would like to be treated—apply? How can someone in the retail or other service industries do a better job of anticipating their customers' needs?

4. Mr. Wade believes that a negative customer experience report can be even more powerful than a word-of-mouth recommendation. Do you agree? Why?

5. Will Jameson learns a lot about why the hotel's guests remain loyal by overhearing a conversation with a guest. Is there a better way to systematically gauge a customer's experience? What are some suggestions?

6. Ari is trying to make the best of a difficult situation by suggesting that his hotel initiate a merger with a chain, despite doubts by his colleague. Is he being realistic? Do you think there are other things he could suggest to management? What might they be?

7. People make a difference by living the vision and mission of the business day in, day out—contributing their ideas, observations, and insights in conversations and meetings, and being a team player. To what extent are team members in your workplace doing this? What can you do to strengthen these behaviors?

8. Anne remarks that she thinks "even the guests sense how bad it has gotten." How fast can a service culture change

from positive to negative? How does a negative atmosphere in one department affect other departments and eventually the entire guest experience?

PART TWO

Chapter 5

Out of Service

The coldest winter I ever saw was the
summer I spent in San Francisco.
—attributed to Mark Twain

The classic sounds of Blood, Sweat, and Tears poured out of the manager's office adjacent to the front desk.

"What goes up, must come down;
Spinnin' wheel, goes 'round and 'round.
Talk 'bout your troubles and you cry in shame.
Ride a painted pony, let the spinnin' wheel spin."

It had been a spinning-wheel kind of summer at the Hotel Metronome. Nobody knew where that wheel was going to land. It had been both unusually hectic and unusually hot. The occupancy rate was at an all-time high (which pleased the parent company), but Will Jameson, Cora, and even Ella Moran were at their wits' end dealing with a multitude of new challenges.

First, it seemed that the cramped and cranky elevator was down for days at a time, leaving many of the elderly guests in the lurch. Damien Townsend almost gave notice after hauling bags and heavy Napa wine-packs up eight floors; only the additional tips kept him on the job. Cora, Caitlin, Damien, and Tim listened patiently day after day as previously loyal guests complained to Reception that they simply couldn't return under such trying conditions.

All this was intensified by the freakishly warm weather in San Francisco. Most summers the room air conditioners were hardly used, but this year they ran nonstop. Guests returning to the hotel sweating and out of breath from their city tours and Union Square walks groused at seeing the elevator with its Out of Service sign posted. Only the free wine hours seemed to placate them—but that was hardly enough.

The always-difficult telephone system vexed a good many guests too, forcing the reception team to spend more time than they wished explaining how to master it. Many guests never received voice-mail messages; a good number of planned meetings, lunches, and dinners never happened because of it.

Director of Guest Services Ella Moran (a.k.a. Cruella to the front desk and housekeeping staffs that reported to her) also managed the restaurant and saw almost constant employee turnover there as more boutique hotels opened and competed for experienced wait people. The kitchen was in the basement, while the hotel's restaurant was just off the lobby on the first floor, adding to the problems.

The dumbwaiter could only handle so much. Without a working service elevator, the wait staff's days became unusually tiresome while the food became cold, making the hospitality mantra "serve hot food hot and cold food cold" very difficult to achieve. Room service was often suspended because the elevator was usually needed to transport carts to the various floors. Guests were unhappy about this, too. It was a *very* difficult time at the Metronome.

"Will, we simply can't run a hotel like this," Ella said to the manager one particularly warm August day. "I have never seen so many surly guests, and it's impacting morale in the restaurant, in housekeeping, in the club lounge, and here at the front desk. The bar seems to be the only refuge for the guests, and then they don't want to stay and eat here because their meals arrive late—and cold to boot. It's just not working. Our service systems are breaking down all around us!"

Cora and Tim both remained silent, astonished that Ella actually took the lead on giving Will his "cancer on the presidency" speech. Customarily she was the most upbeat of anybody on the staff, at least for the benefit of the clientele, and here she was appointing herself as the spokesperson for the disenchanted.

"You know, she's right, Will," Damien chimed in reluctantly. "We have gone from having one of the most positive staffs in the area to one of the most negative. Every day we get calls from upcoming guests who ask whether the elevator is working. When we admit that we're having problems again, they cancel and reserve elsewhere. It really is a major deal for a lot of people. And it's difficult for me, too—bigger tips or not."

Cora finally added her two cents.

"When people ask me to recommend restaurants to them, of course I suggest they eat right here in Tempus Fugit. The food is delicious, and a real value for San Francisco. Lots of them counter by saying it isn't well run, but they don't know about the logistics problem with the kitchen in the basement. It isn't Ella's fault, but she often gets the blame. She takes it well and tries to explain the problem, but people just don't care. They want things to be corrected. Ask some of the guests themselves, Will. You know Mr. Wade is here again, for the thirtieth-some-odd time. Ask him what he thinks about the hotel these days. You know he never complains about anything, but we've noticed he isn't smiling and chatting with us so much anymore. When your best and most loyal customers abandon the flock, you've got to do something pretty radical."

Cora started to feel that they were ganging up on Will, but Ella had more to say.

"Just last night one of the newlywed couples in the hotel were looking forward to the romantic dinner they were supposed to receive as part of their wedding package here," she said. "They walked in all lovey-dovey, waited nearly forty-five minutes for their food, and then decided to go somewhere else. We were so busy we just couldn't expedite their dinners fast enough. They didn't say anything, but their faces told the story. They were not happy. They could easily post something nasty on the Internet. You know, more and more people are doing that. It's impacting the housekeeping staff too, you know, as they are sometimes the first line of defense when a guest is unhappy. Their English-language skills are sometimes not the best, and even though they are just about the cheeriest staff I have ever had to manage, they can only do so much."

Will had had enough. From the little office just to the right of the reception desk, he, too, heard comments regularly about problems in the hotel. He knew that when people stayed at lifestyle hotels like the Metronome or even mid-price, full-service hotels, they generally tolerated problems more than those who opted for the five-star hotels like the Ritz-Carlton or the Four Seasons, where everything was expected to be perfect. But regardless, he didn't enjoy hearing about *any* guests dissatisfied with their stay. If they were to live up to their vision and mission, they would have to begin making some important changes—and soon!

"Okay, okay, folks," he responded, throwing up his hands in mock surrender. "You've made your points. I didn't realize how much you were being impacted. I'll take the blame because I have been reluctant to go to our parent company and ask for major improvements to be made here. They are in acquisitions mode right now, and cash is in short supply. But this is threatening our very survival. The occupancy rates haven't been affected *yet*, but I notice that you guys at the front desk are having to apologize for things to make sure that doesn't become a problem too. I am going to ask for an elevator upgrade, a new phone and voice-mail system, a reservations system that shows availability at our sister hotels, new flat-screen computers for the business center, additional electronic equipment for the meeting rooms, and a lobby renovation. Anything else you can think of for our wish list?"

The four employees looked at each other, hesitant to push Will any further.

"Well, while you're at it," Ella said demurely, "might as well ask for upgraded air conditioners. If the ones we have now break down later this summer or next, people are going to be steamed, in more ways than one. But if you want to get some totally objective feedback from our best customer, Henry Wade is having lunch in our restaurant right now."

———

As shifts changed, Cora couldn't wait to tell Caitlin about the ambush of the general manager.

"I was shocked that Ella stood her ground," Cora said conspiratorially under her breath. "You know how she's always been the good soldier around here. I couldn't believe she may be one of us after all. You should have seen her."

Caitlin remained dubious. She and Ella had a history of feuds between them. "Don't trust Cruella," Caitlin snapped. "There is only one person she cares about, and that's herself. I have gone to the mat too many times with her, and she has proven time and again that she's going to be the victor, one way or another."

"Cait, sweetie, people change," Cora rejoined. "I always think good things come out of adversity. After the recent hard time here, maybe this is the good that's going to occur thanks to us sticking it out and speaking up. And maybe Ella is figuring it out too. Let's give her the benefit of the doubt. It doesn't cost anything to do that."

"Cora, we all love you, but I've always thought you were just a little too naive, too ready to forgive and move on. I don't think people like her ever change. She has huge issues and wants to be loved by everyone, at everyone else's cost. It's happened to you a dozen times, and now you say for us to forgive and forget. You must be a better person than I am, because I just can't do that so easily."

Tim Olmos had rushed in, late and out of breath as usual, but heard enough of their conversation to be able to contribute his own thoughts on the matter.

"I had been thinking of talking to Will about the issues around here too, but you both know that this is just a job for me. I do it to pay the bills. My photography is what I really care about."

"Yeah, we both know that, Tim," Cora said for the hundredth time, "but our guests should never get that sense. They haven't until now because I think you really *do* care, your photographs aside. They love your sarcasm, your playfulness, your personality—*and* your ability to invest that little bit extra with each guest. You have turned a lot of people around lately who have had to walk down those stairs in the morning with sleep in their eyes, ready to set the place on fire. Everybody has a right to pass on their thoughts to management, and I for one am glad that Ella had the courage to do it. She gets special bonus points from me. I'm not sure we've been fair to her."

The Ninety-Second Rule

Invest just ninety seconds more with each guest whenever possible by

1. reading the guest for time availability;
2. asking open-ended questions;
3. drilling down for further insights when in conversations with the guest;
4. assessing how the guest really is feeling about what he or she is telling you; and
5. using active listening to check your understanding of his or her message.

Tim and Caitlin rolled their eyes at each other before Tim spoke.

"Okay, Corazon, I'll give her another chance. But she has made my own life difficult on more than one occasion. She is going to have to prove herself in my book. One more trip to get things for guests, and I'll wring her skinny neck."

"You'll do no such thing," Cora said, smiling slightly at the image of Ella's neck in Tim's hands. "In fact, I predict that before the summer is over, you are going to be apologizing to her for misjudging her motives. Just you watch."

"Well, *I* certainly won't," Caitlin snapped, never easy to convince about anything. "I'll quit before I ever do that. People don't change, Cora. They don't. Just you wait, and then you can buy me lunch when you finally realize it."

———

Questions for Group Discussion

1. The Metronome has been going through a difficult period. Has your own company had to endure downturns in business? Recall a time when your own company or department experienced a business setback. How did management handle it? How did the employees? If you were the manager, what would you have done differently?

2. Cora talks about what happens when loyal customers "abandon the flock." Have you seen that happen in your own company? Did anyone notice? What was done?

3. Cora tells Caitlin that Ella may be "one of us" after all. What does she mean? Can an employee be so loyal to management that he or she becomes myopic toward problems within the organization? Have you seen this happen in your own workplace? When and under what circumstances?

4. Caitlin advises Cora not to trust Ella's intentions. What roles do trust and betrayal play in a workplace? Have you

seen the best intentions undermined by lack of trust? How do you build trust? How do you lose it? Explain.

5. All three of the desk staff mention difficulties dealing with change, both in one's personal life and at work. Have you witnessed those difficulties firsthand? In your experience, can people change after all? How difficult do you think it is?

6. When systems and equipment such as telephones and elevators break down, the staff is stretched to their limits— sometimes beyond. What has been your experience with breakdowns in your hotel, restaurant, or service unit? How have these affected you? Your team? What feelings and emotions erupted? How did management respond?

7. Damien states, "We have gone from having one of the most positive staffs in the area to one of the most negative." How easy is it to go from having positive to negative morale? What changes have to happen for this to occur? Have you ever experienced a severe dip in morale where you worked? What happened? Be prepared to discuss your experience with others.

8. What do you think of Tim Olmos's comment, "This is just a job for me. I do it to pay the bills?" How do customers feel when someone they encounter has little or no enthusiasm for his or her job?

Chapter 6

To Everything, There Is a Season

Half our life is spent trying to find something to do with
the time we have rushed through life trying to save.
—Will Rogers

The three noisy and out-of-sync metronomes created quite a
cacophony in the bar area of the lobby, but Henry Wade found
them oddly comforting after a long day at the printer. He knew
that the hotel was not the same as before, but for him it remained
a home away from home. Even more importantly, he felt that the
hotel was almost an extension of his own lifestyle. Despite the
superficial problems, Henry Wade felt confident that the staff and
management would pull together to return things to their former
status. The Englishman walked to the side mirror to adjust his
purple-striped bow tie, which didn't need adjusting at all.

"Would you care for chardonnay or merlot, Mr. Wade?" the
sultry bartender asked. "We're pouring both tonight."

Henry Wade delayed his response when through the mirror he saw Will Jameson approaching behind the colorfully lit liquor bottles.

"Doesn't have to be wine, Mr. Wade. Whatever you want, it's on the house," the general manager said. "I looked for you all afternoon yesterday. Ella said you were in the restaurant for lunch, but I must have missed you."

"Call me Henry, please. Your staff won't."

Henry Wade ordered a Tanqueray and tonic, his favorite warm-weather drink, from Tamara, his bartender of choice after staying there so many times.

"And please call me Will," the hotel manager said. "Seems like we should have had a drink together a long time ago. We really value your loyalty, you know. Loyal customers are the bread and butter of just about any business, but particularly the hospitality industry. We are most appreciative."

"It's nice that you notice. And I am thankful to you too, Will. I always feel welcome here, which is why I come back. But I have to tell you that lunch didn't exactly work out yesterday; my guest and I had to go around the corner because it was taking so long. Not to complain, but I have noticed a few things are a bit rough around the edges lately. That new restaurant of yours has some real issues, as I'm sure you must know."

"I think I know, but I'd love to hear about them from your own point of view."

Henry Wade spoke carefully, staring straight into Will Jameson's eyes. Neither man blinked.

"I hope you don't mind if I am completely candid, Will. I have always been fairly easy to please, I think. I have never even changed rooms in a hotel, and I travel quite a lot. My standards are high, but consistency is even more important. I don't like surprises, and until the last couple of times here, I never found any. The staff is uniformly delightful, and I love being greeted like a paterfamilias every time I arrive."

Will Jameson listened intently, waiting for the inevitable "but." It didn't take long.

"But the last couple of visits, I have noticed the attention to detail that I always remarked upon to my colleagues in England seems to be lacking. It's not just the elevator either, though that ongoing problem has affected quite a few people. Your guests don't express the usual sunny disposition I have come to expect and which I enjoy seeing after a stressful day. I enjoy coming down here to the lobby and overhearing their conversations, but lately they don't seem to linger like they used to. The staff seems demoralized, and their demeanor appears forced. Cora is the only one on the front desk who always makes the best of it. She's definitely the bright spot around here. The others, however, seem cynical—even defeated. I am sure you are well aware of the subliminal message an attitude like that sends to your guests. It's critical to address an issue like that, which can be easily fixed—unlike the situation with the lift, I mean elevator."

Will seemed almost defeated himself. He wanted to offer a defense, but he knew it would likely come up short.

"Henry, we value you so much as a customer, as a member of the family really, so I am going to pay special attention to what you have told me. Please don't judge us too harshly during this difficult time. The parent company has put a lot of faith in us while they have been acquiring other hotels. Give us three to six months, and I can guarantee you all the things that are important to you will be at least examined. You have been with us a long time, through thick and thin, and I really hope you can stick with us during this lean period. My staff gave me some hard feedback just yesterday, and it made me see things in a different light."

"I admire what you are trying to do here, Will. I don't need any special treatment. I don't need flowers in my room or a bottle of champagne when I arrive. I just want to be comfortable and made to feel like I matter. And, once again, I don't like surprises. I think that's fairly universal in what people need and expect. Pay more attention to what people are saying about their experiences on the various travel sites. You might be surprised."

Will Jameson stopped to evaluate before responding. He was not accustomed to such a rational argument when dealing with guests, especially the most loyal ones.

"That's really good advice, Henry. I sometimes get too busy to ask guests about their time here. We are on the same page. I so value your candid feedback and will do whatever I can to make your stay particularly memorable, even under difficult circumstances. I hope you know that on your next stay here, we would be delighted to offer you a complimentary weekend at the penthouse level. That's the least we can do."

Henry Wade thought about it for a microsecond before responding. "Oh, great," he said, smiling. "That means walking up yet another flight of stairs! I think I'll pass."

———

Music aficionado Ari Libman ratcheted his iPod up to max volume to hear the Lovin' Spoonful's take on the hazy and humid New York weather everyone was *kvetching* about yet suffering through:

"Hot town, summer in the city;
Back of my neck getting dirty and gritty.
Been down, isn't it a pity?
Doesn't seem to be a shadow in the city.

All around, people looking half-dead ...
Walking on the sidewalk, hotter than a match head."

He decided to sit on the front stoop to wait for his colleague Anne Livingston to arrive. Things had improved at the Hotel Metro, so he didn't mind listening to her almost-constant complaining. Now she had the heat to contend with rather than management.

"Ari, what are you doing out here?" Anne called and waved from nearly half a block away. "It's filthy hot out here. Are you out of your mind?"

Some things never changed, and Anne's attitude was one of them.

"Hi, sweetie. You're early for once." He knew he was going to have to joke with her to endure this sweltering evening in the concrete city.

"Yeah, the chick teaching our Pilates class was not feeling well, so we got out of there pronto," Anne said. "I needed some relaxation after that awful day at work."

"What are you talking about? Pilates is relaxation to you?"

"Yes, it is, as a matter of fact. You should try it. You could use some stress relief, too, you know."

Ari recalled that his friend Cora in San Francisco had mentioned in one of their phone calls how Pilates had helped her wind down as well. *I really should call her,* Ari thought. *It would be nice to tell her that things at work have improved, mostly because of her advice.*

"Oh, did I tell you?" Anne asked suddenly. "Our boss, Dale, asked me if I wanted to organize a 10K run in October with people from the hotel. It would benefit breast cancer research. He's been much nicer to me lately, but you know it takes a while to earn my trust. I don't know what you did, but it worked."

Ari didn't know exactly how it happened, but Dale Rothman had actually listened to him sometime in April about being acquired by a small boutique hotel chain based in Canada. The deal had not yet closed, but Dale had allowed Ari to proofread the press release, so he knew it was on the verge of happening. He and Dale had even forged a relationship of sorts, and Anne was benefiting as well.

"Hey, mister. You're not paying any attention to me," Anne whined. "I can go home to Oscar and get better treatment. What are you thinking about anyway?"

Ari contemplated the question. How could he summarize everything that was in his mind for this woman who had such issues?

"Annie, I never told you, but I was on the verge of quitting the Metro a few months ago. It was making me too negative. But I took my friend Cora's advice about speaking up to management, and look what's happened. Not only do I have Dale singing my praises, but they changed some policies and we're getting great reviews in the local media. They spent some money on upgrading the website, and we're almost full—even during the week. Did Dale tell you the new owners are thinking about buying the deli next door and turning it into the hotel restaurant?"

"Get out!" Anne shrieked, mimicking Elaine Benes on *Seinfeld*. "I'll believe it when I see it."

Building Relationships
1. Communicate openly and honestly.
2. Always treat people with courtesy, dignity, and respect.
3. Develop binding trust.
4. Never lose sight of the vision to make people happy.
5. Recovery strategies can save your life and that of the organization.

"Honey, things are changing for the better, and you still have doubts. When are you going to get on board?"

"Mr. Libman," as Anne called him when she wanted to add extra emphasis or whenever she felt he was getting too full of himself, "I'll get on board when I trust that management is going to treat me right. Dale is being pretty nice these days, but he and they have a long way to go after all they've done to me in the past. Trust is a two-way street."

"Annie, past is past. Let's look at the future for once."

———

Questions for Group Discussion

1. The Metronome's manager says that loyal customers are the bread and butter of just about any business. Do you agree? How can companies do a better job of creating loyalty?

2. Henry Wade talks about the subliminal message that is sent out to customers when employees are unhappy. Have you experienced that, either as a worker or as a customer? How did it impact you?

3. "I just want to be comfortable and made to feel like I matter," Henry Wade says. Is that a universal feeling? Have you ever felt that way yourself? When?

4. Henry reinforces his point about not liking surprises. Except for birthdays, most people do not like surprises; employees don't like management by surprise, and guests

don't like inconsistencies in what they are paying for. How do you feel when you are surprised about something unexpected? How do you think guests feel when they experience unexpected surprises?

5. Anne states, "You know it takes a while to earn my trust." Often referred to as the bedrock of relationships, trust is a very fragile component of meaningful relationship building. How important is trust to you? What are your expectations from others? Do most companies care about their employees' trust factors? Why or why not?

Chapter 7

All I Want for Christmas ...

The pessimist sees difficulty in every opportunity. The
optimist sees the opportunity in every difficulty.
—Winston Churchill

Two elderly women, first-timers at the Metronome, stepped
gingerly from the sixth-floor landing into the newly
refurbished elevator. They had heard the stories about its quirks
and didn't want to aggravate it in any way.

It was barely seven thirty on the Saturday morning before
Christmas when they were transported downstairs without
incident, ready to take on the day. They had checked into the hotel
late the previous afternoon but had already taken in a number of
San Francisco's sights, including Fisherman's Wharf, Union Square,
and the Embarcadero. The demure, overly made-up ladies had even
ridden the famous cable cars—twice. Their experience on the F
Market streetcar was not as pleasant, as a number of the city's more
colorful (and profane) residents enjoyed shocking tourists with
their boisterous misbehavior. It was the first time these southern

ladies had ever seen a man in a dress, unless one included San Francisco's resident celebrity, Robin Williams, in *Mrs. Doubtfire*.

Ella Moran was just unlocking the main doors to the Tempus Fugit restaurant when the ladies migrated from the empty lobby for a light Continental breakfast. Always budget-conscious, they were determined to maximize their vacation dollars by taking advantage of the all-inclusives their travel agent had promised.

"Good morning, ladies," Ella chirped, smiling broadly. "You are up early for a Saturday morning. You must have a full day planned."

"We do, we most certainly do," the taller of the two said in a delightful southern drawl. "When you're on holiday, we think you are wasting time staying in your room all day."

"Couldn't agree more," Ella responded, pushing open the French doors to the restaurant, "especially in a beautiful city like ours. Where would you like to sit? The place is all yours."

The two women consulted each other before deciding on a table in the front bow window. The early morning sun streamed through. It promised a nice start to what had been predicted to be a cool late-December day in San Francisco. Both had packed for a variety of weather scenarios after consulting numerous travel guides that warned about the city's topsy-turvy climate.

"Would you like coffee or tea?" Ella asked. "I'm the manager but will do double duty until your server gets everything set up. Most of our guests sleep in on Saturdays."

"Oh my goodness. Are we too early? We can take a walk around the block and come back," one said.

"Yes, let's do that. They're not ready for us," said the second.

Ella shifted into low gear. She loved customer challenges like this.

"Don't be silly, girls. Coffee is freshly made, and we always have hot water ready for tea. Which will you have? I'll bring it while you look over these menus, but I suspect you prefer your coffee strong and black."

The ladies giggled. They didn't realize it, but they were being teased by a real hotel professional.

"That's us. We're sisters—I'm Rose, and she's Violet—and we've both been drinking coffee since we were babies. Our momma and daddy thought it was good for us. We actually made some in the room earlier, but I'll bet yours is much better."

"Coming right up," Ella said. "Check out the menus, and I'll be back to take your order. If you are simply looking for a Continental breakfast, that's included in your room rate. If you would like anything more, you'll need to order à la carte."

Ella went to see if the coffee had finished brewing while the sisters consulted their menus.

"I'm fine with a Continental breakfast," Rose whispered. "Then we can have a nice lunch and not be too full for the party tonight. We should take advantage of the package after all."

Violet had other ideas.

"You know how I love bacon, Rose, and they have that Applewood smoked bacon out here. Remember that piano student of mine, Jimmy Ray Butler? Well, his momma sent me some as a thank-you present once. I'll have the Continental breakfast too, but I must have some bacon on the side. I don't care what it costs. Even if it's five dollars, it's worth it to me. I've been thinking about it since we started planning this trip."

"Honey chile, that's the cost of a whole breakfast in Jackson," Rose admonished. Rose had always had that "powerfully sad streak of frugality" in her, as Violet called it.

Ella returned with a fresh pot of coffee in her hand and poured a cup for each of the sisters. "Okay, ladies, what will it be? I'm ready."

"But I thought you said you were the manager," Rose said with some concern in her voice. "We can wait 'til the help gets here."

"No, no. We're all 'the help' here. We all are team players and help each other out as we go. We just want to make it easy on our guests. If you ladies would like to get an early start on seeing the city, then we're here for you."

The elderly women looked at each other, somewhat perplexed but obviously pleased nonetheless.

Rose ordered first. "That's sweet of you. Then I'll just have the Continental breakfast with sourdough toast—buttered, apple juice, and the coffee. If you have some honey for the toast, that would be nice too."

Violet had barely looked at the menu. "I'll have biscuits and molasses with a side of that smoked bacon. Oops—I meant smoked bacon on the side," she said, giggling again. A side of bacon might have been more than even a pork aficionado could have handled.

Ella decided she was going to have fun with these delightful ladies from the South. She wrongly guessed Georgia or Alabama as their birthplace instead of Mississippi and wondered to herself if they had gloves upstairs for church the next day.

"I'm sorry; we don't have biscuits on the menu. But right around the corner and just about a half block down the hill, right on the cable car line, there's a famous breakfast place that has southern-style biscuits and gravy that they serve all day. I can have somebody run and get you an order if you aren't in a rush, and you can have them right here. They probably even have molasses. We aim to please. If a guest asks for something we don't have, we find a way to get it for them."

The sisters seemed a little embarrassed. They now understood why their travel agent had been so insistent on the Metronome for this splurge trip, despite the higher prices.

"Oh, don't bother about that," Violet said, fussing with her napkin. "We can visit there tomorrow maybe. I'll just have the Continental like my sister and that order of bacon. I saw a woman once in the Dairy Queen with a T-shirt that said, 'Men are pigs, but I love bacon.' I couldn't agree more." Both women laughed uproariously, and Ella found herself joining in the merriment.

The Metronome's renovation of its public spaces had not been effortless. Completed, everyone agreed that it had been long overdue and was well worth the wait. The three-month schedule promised by the contractor went by the wayside, but the result was so successful that nobody complained—neither guests nor staff. Even the parent company, with offices just down the street, agreed that the hotel was beautifully restored without being ostentatious.

The confrontation between Will Jameson and Ella Moran back in August, complemented by the support of Ella by her employees, turned out to be a harbinger of better staff relations to come. Tim Olmos stopped calling her Cruella; Damien Townsend started inviting her to his garage-band gigs at the Purple Onion on Polk Street (with its blinking neon martini glass); and even Tamara, the wine-hour bartender, began bringing Ella Virgin Mary's every afternoon, knowing that Ella, a professional to the core, would never tipple on the job. Only Caitlin Gold held onto her doubts about their supervisor. But even she was beginning to crumble.

The dumbwaiter delivered the sisters' meals almost too quickly, for Ella hoped to chat them up a bit more. She liked these ladies, almost personifications of the slow, gracious South that was on the verge of being lost today. Ella was a product of it herself, but had kept her personal life private to just about everybody. *Oh, but for a return to those times of gentleness and charm,* she thought. *What has happened to our world?*

She took the breakfast tray from the dumbwaiter and set it on the service stand just across from them. They remained the only guests in the restaurant.

"Here you are, ladies. I found some special clover honey for your toast and shook a little cinnamon into your apple juice. Would you care for more coffee?"

"Oh, no, honey. You are spoiling us. We haven't been treated this nicely since we went to New York City last spring."

In the movies they would call it a double take. Ella couldn't believe these two could ever have found their way to Manhattan, much less enjoyed its demanding pace.

"You, um, took a trip to New York City last year—and enjoyed it?" Ella asked incredulously. She personally loved New York but found it rather daunting. If only she had a friend there who could show her around, maybe it would be less so. Maybe Cora could introduce her to the fellow she had met on the train whom she always talked about. Cora told Ella several times she was going to try to get him to come out to San Francisco.

Violet spread honey on her sourdough toast.

"Oh my word. We had the best time in the world there. We stayed at a hotel near Times Square that wasn't nearly as nice as this, but we met a charming young Jewish boy there who worked at the front desk. People say New Yorkers are rude and aggressive, but we thought they were wonderful. On the streets, we never even looked at a map without somebody asking if we needed directions. The man at the front desk even took us on the subway with him when he got off work to accompany us to an Italian restaurant in Greenwich Village, where we were meeting our grandniece. If they ever give out an award for Friendliest City, it would be New York. And so far we are finding the same in San Francisco."

The lightbulb went off in Ella's head. She paused and reflected for a moment, wondering if such a wild coincidence could actually be possible.

"I think I know which hotel you are talking about, ladies. Is it the Metro?"

"Oh my goodness! You're right. How'd you know? That sweet young desk clerk made our whole trip."

"Can you believe the lovely Filipina woman at our own front desk is friends with him? They met on a train when she was visiting family in the East. Isn't it a small world?"

"It is when you get to talking with people," Violet said. "So many people never slow down enough to engage and actually talk with one another. Conversation is becoming a lost art. That's why I always travel with my sister. We never run out of things to say to each other."

For once in her life, Ella was speechless. She quickly walked the fifteen steps to get the coffeepot, shaking her head in the process.

"I'm glad you are enjoying yourselves, ladies. If there's anything I or anyone on my staff can do to help you out—answer questions, snap a souvenir picture, make reservations, anything—just let me know. How did you find this hotel anyway?"

"We have a friend who's a part-time travel agent," Rose said, "and she suggested this hotel. Violet and I are two of three girls, and we're here for our third sister's fiftieth wedding anniversary. She got the pretty name—Dahlia Mae. Everybody calls her Dolly. She lives in Oakland, so we're going to take the subway over there tonight. We knew we wanted something special for her party, but we had never been to San Francisco so we wanted to stay in the city instead of across the Bay in Oakland."

"That's right," Violet echoed. "Our friend took us down to her basement, where she runs her business, and she read us all the customer comments on the Internet that people had made about this hotel. She even showed us pictures of the rooms. We couldn't believe you could see where you were going to be sleeping in a couple of months! Your rates were more than we wanted to spend, but those customer comments convinced us. The only negative ones were about your elevator, but our friend called here and somebody assured her that you had replaced it. And you know what? You and your staff have confirmed all those nice comments. Those two on the front desk joked with us when we were checking in yesterday and recommended a place for dinner last night just down the street. They really seemed to know what we would like."

That would be Cora and Tim, Ella thought. *They're better at what they do than I give them credit for. They never lost their sense of humor during the renovation and smoothed things over with more than a few irate guests. I am going to say something to Will about giving them a couple of gift certificates. They deserve it.*

"I am so pleased to hear you say that," she said to the southern ladies. "You must be the Truitt sisters on the sixth floor. I heard about your arrival yesterday. Tim, the desk agent who checked you in, said you were lovely and very funny. I should have figured it out earlier."

"Oh, that boy is a sweetheart. He and the young woman on the desk had quite a time putting us on. They made us laugh so hard. It looks to me like they might have something going on," Violet said, winking at Rose. "Every man needs a good woman in his life." Rose nodded in agreement.

Ella hesitated a moment before answering, discreetly, "I think the good woman in his life is probably his mother."

The Saturday morning breakfast guests began trickling in, eager to get a head start on Christmas shopping for friends and family far away. A line outside the restaurant's door had developed. Ella was still alone and scurrying a little faster than normal when Caitlin Gold poked her head into the cafe around the corner from the reception desk.

"Ella, Chris just called and said she's having problems getting in. The BART [Bay Area Rapid Transit] is running way behind schedule because of some signal problems. Do you need some help in here? It's pretty slow right now, so Damien can cover the front desk for a few minutes," said Caitlin. "It's a good thing we talked about cross-training in the department staff meeting last month, don't you think?"

"Yes, I do, Cait, and some help would be great," Ella said, more harried than usual. "Seat the guests and pour them some coffee or tea. You know the drill."

Damien took his post at the front desk while the two women worked like a well-engineered machine, efficiently getting the guests their badly needed morning caffeine fixes. Nobody would have guessed there had ever been serious issues between them.

Best Practices for Team Players

1. Have an attitude of being a part of everything, rather than being apart from everything.
2. Focus on each team member's strengths.
3. Contribute to team successes by adding value to all guest interactions in everything you say and do.
4. Maligning guests or other team members outside their presence is against the rules.
5. Know, understand, and administer the organization's Kool-Aid.

The Truitt sisters vacated their table so that Ella and Caitlin could seat a party of four there, waving to Ella as they left. "We'll see you later, hon," Rose said. "Thank you for everything."

"If I don't see you, have fun at your sister's celebration tonight, ladies," Ella said in response.

"Those women make me smile," Caitlin said as she put together a pair of two-tops for the family in 518. "I hope I'm as spry and positive when I'm their age. They really inspire you, don't you think?"

"Oh my goodness, yes," Ella responded on her way to the dumbwaiter to pick up another breakfast order. "If I had their energy and love of life, my problems would be over."

"I never thought you had problems, Ella. You have so many secrets. But here, let me deliver those," Caitlin said to the woman they had all dissected so many times. Taking the tray of breakfasts, she added, "I feel cheated that you're getting all the fun customers. Mine are a little surly today."

"Thanks, sweetie. They're probably just victims of the holiday season. It puts a lot of people in a bad mood. My advice is be careful how you deal with them. Give them a little Christmas cheer, and I'll bet they'll warm up to you."

"Gosh, Ella, I guess I've never seen you in action in here," Caitlin said. "You really know how to 'work the room.' I never knew."

"Well," said Ella, "the secret is in the attitude of trying to be aware of what is going on in the entire room so you can help out where needed. I use my peripheral vision or the corners of my eyes to keep a handle on what's happening, so when a guest needs something, they rarely even have to ask for it. Anticipation is my middle name."

Ella began to make her fifth pot of coffee while Caitlin maneuvered a cart of dirty dishes down to the kitchen in the basement. The new ramp installed during the lobby renovation, however steep, meant they didn't have to commandeer the elevator anymore. *This kitchen and restaurant arrangement is still inefficient,* Caitlin thought, *but what an improvement over before! And I'm actually enjoying stepping up to help the team. Have I drunk the Kool-Aid or what?*

The Saturday before Christmas meant little to Ari Libman, though he never failed to get caught up in the awe of it all. *Christmas in New York City, beautifully lit up in lights, would excite anyone,* he thought—*whatever one's religious beliefs.* The Metro's guests routinely asked for directions to the Rockefeller Center tree just a few blocks away. Many wanted to know whether SoHo was still the hot outdoor shopping mall it once was, and many more only cared about which way to turn to get to Macy's just around the corner. The younger guests had heard that Santa Claus maintained a Wonderland on the seventh floor there.

Gripped in an arctic blast that week, New Yorkers and hotel guests both bundled up. Jewish or not, observant or not, wrapped in lamb's wool or not, Ari was happy to be a part of the holiday experience for the Metro's guests. He and Anne Livingston had united to become a formidable team at the front desk since their manager, Dale Rothman, had hired a new concierge and two new porters to augment Guest Services. Ari and Anne, as well as the new concierge, fielded constant requests for inside information about Times Square, Broadway, Chinatown, Radio City Music Hall, and even the hot Chelsea art galleries not far away. The hotel had definitely recovered from the dog days of summer. Ari wondered how his friend Cora in San Francisco was coping with the season. *Christmas must be very different in a semitropical climate,* he thought.

They probably decorate the palm trees out there. I really should call her. She's the reason I felt confident enough to challenge the powers that be around here.

Anne Livingston arrived with watery eyes and a red, dripping nose, barely suppressing a massive sneeze. Ari felt lucky that he had so far escaped any major bacteria-driven illnesses. It was amazing with people in such close proximity in the enormous city that everybody wasn't confined to bed in their often tiny apartments.

"Why didn't you stay home today, doll?" Ari asked, genuinely concerned about his friend and colleague's health. "Do you want to spread this around? Why do people feel so obligated to come to work when they're clearly supposed to be drinking OJ and eating soup?"

"Only Jews say *eating* soup," she responded in a nasally voice. "The rest of us say *drinking*. I didn't want to leave you here alone. Plus, I don't want to be in the apartment with that nutty parrot whistling at me all day." She mimicked the wolf whistle she heard constantly whenever Oscar was awake. "Why can't it be construction workers?" she asked.

"Put a sheet over that pervert," Ari said. He had never been a fan of Oscar. "You're probably not going to get a boyfriend with that bird around."

"Oh, shush, you. I love Oscar. I had to add a special section in my will because he is probably going to outlive me by far."

"Oooh, that's creepy," Ari said. "Don't leave him to me! Remember that scene with the parakeet in *What Ever Happened to Baby Jane?*"

"Now you're grossing me out. It's supposed to be the holiday season. Behave!"

The phone at the desk rang. Anne slid a finger across her throat to indicate that Ari should answer. Her voice was in tatters.

"Hotel Metro front desk. Ari speaking. How may I help you?"

Cora Tyler had decided weeks ago her Jewish friend in New York needed a little holiday cheer. She even sent him a menorah to brighten his spirits.

"I have been thinking about you *so* much," Cora said into the phone. "We have all these guests from New York who are trying to escape the holidays there. What is the matter with them? Is it just the harsh winter? I see reports on the nightly news, and it looks so beautiful. I wish I were there. How are you doing? I know it's not a major holiday for you, but I hope you are coping. Being single and Jewish can't be easy for you."

Ari was truly touched. People almost never understood his reticence about celebrating the holiday. Many Jews in New York felt a real ambivalence about Christmas. He was one of them.

"Oh, sweetie. Don't worry about me," he told her. "Christmas is beautiful here no matter what religion you are. The hotel is full of people of all faiths, and they just love it, especially the kids. Don't you think it has become a secular holiday really?"

"Yeah, I do, but I'm kind of sad about that. As my twins get older, I wonder about what lies in store for them because of the religious conflicts in the world. I wish everybody could live in harmony. We have two elderly southern sisters staying here, and they would say, 'Oh, shut my mouth'—so I will. I'm sorry to be so serious. I wish I could be there with you."

"Oh, Cora. Things are so much better here now, mostly thanks to you. I don't want to be all mealymouthed about it, as our own southern guests would say, but you really opened my eyes about how we process information. I am in a much happier place now. I understand the big picture better, and I am working on building our service culture every day. My friend Anne has come a long way, too. But how are things there?"

Cora hesitated a moment. She had heard that Caitlin and Ella had finally found a way to deal with their differences, but that had taken some time. Should she tone down her enthusiasm for the way things had played out over the past few months, difficulties aside? She didn't want Ari to think she was too namby-pamby.

"Ari, honestly, it has been a tough time here, particularly during the renovation," she said cautiously, "but management has been fair and honest about where we were going and what might happen, as far as they knew. We all were willing to go on the magic carpet ride with them, even though we didn't know where we were going to land. That's the key—having faith that the landing is going to be a soft one. I think we all learned that management has the same issues we do; they're just as fearful of articulating them as we are about hearing them. Managers are supposed to have all the answers, and when they don't, they think they've failed. We're lucky to have a management team, including those in the corporate offices down the street, who are willing to admit that they are just as vulnerable as the staff. But our manager here inspires us to go along with him on the ride. That's true leadership in my book, and, sadly, people don't recognize it because they so seldom see it."

Cora surprised herself. She had never spoken about business and management and leadership issues quite like that. Would Ari laugh at her? Could he relate? She really didn't know.

"Honey, you say it so well. You know that I've had big doubts about the way things have gone here at the hotel, but I have put my faith into the future and it has paid off. My friend Anne is still questioning, aren't you, Annie?" he said as he looked at her, still sniffling. "But I'm convinced that you get what you put into it. Doesn't seem such a leap after all, does it?"

Cora didn't want to sound like someone management had bought off, but she *did* feel strongly about her own values and beliefs and how they were in sync with the core values and practices of the hotel. It sounded as if Ari was finally embracing them.

"No, you're wrong, buddy. It *is* a leap. It represents an enormous, dangerous chasm for a lot of people. It's the Grand Canyon for many. It's taken you almost a year to come to these conclusions for yourself, but you sound sincere in what you've come to discover. I'm really happy for you. It's the best Christmas gift I could have ever wished for."

"And I didn't even send you one," Ari said, chastising himself. "Next year, I promise. But I hope to see you before then, either on this coast or yours."

"You don't even celebrate the holiday," Cora replied, "but I hope you enjoy it anyway. How's about we try for a Passover date instead? That would be a special gift, and I am dying to try *kugel*. I hear it's delicious. I'll have the chef make up a special batch for all our Passover guests."

"You mean me, right?" Ari asked, grinning at Anne.

Cora smiled too. "That would be a 'Yes,' Mr. Libman."

————

Questions for Group Discussion

1.   1. Ella tells the southern ladies, "We aim to please. If a guest asks for something we don't have, we find a way to get it for them." Is that realistic in today's service environment? Can a company or business be *too* customer-centric?

2.   Interpersonal relationships have improved after Ella's straightforward confrontation with her boss. Have you seen that happen at your own company? What risks does an employee take by being direct?

3. Caitlin wonders if she has "drunk the Kool-Aid." What does she mean? What do coworkers think of people who have drunk the organization's Kool-Aid?

4. Ari talks about how we process information. To what extent do you think attitude plays in the outcome of certain things? What could you do to examine the role of attitude in processing information?

5. Cora counsels Ari on how management can be just as fearful of the unknown as employees are. Do you think that is true? How can management do a better job of articulating their vision of the future? What do employees need to do a better job of getting on board? How can this best be accomplished?

6. "We're all 'the help' here. We all ... help each other out as we go," stated Ella. Successful teams follow this service principle, sometimes referred to as "lateral service." Identify situations in which you have helped out other team members and they you. What did you think? How did you feel?

7. "If a guest asks for something we don't have, we find a way to get it for them." Think of examples in which you or others have gone the "extra mile" to ensure a guest's satisfaction. Share them in your group discussions.

8. How often do you think guests read customer comments on the web before they book a hotel? What impact does this have on reputation and reservations?

9. Cora is the reason Ari felt confident enough to "challenge the powers that be." How confident are you in voicing your opinion so that it is taken with a positive attitude and as a constructive suggestion? Identify examples.

10. "Managers are supposed to have all the answers, and when they don't, they think they've failed." Discuss this statement in light of your thinking and experiences. What can you do to ensure situations become a win-win for everyone?

Chapter 8

Back to the Future

Happiness is a continuation of happenings which are not resisted.
—Deepak Chopra

The trip to JFK airport proved to be the most challenging part of Ari Libman's journey to the San Francisco Bay Area. The Metropolitan Transit Authority's new AirTrain, years in the planning, made it easier on the wallet, but it meant nearly an hour on the subway just getting to it. Ari had been telling Anne how important it was to leave "a light footprint on the planet," so he felt it would be disingenuous not to use mass transit whenever he could. He even made special arrangements to take BART, the Bay area's subway system, into San Francisco once he landed in Oakland, just across the peninsula from the city where Tony Bennett left his heart.

As he settled into the aisle seat on his first JetBlue flight, Ari reflected on what had brought him into Cora Tyler's orbit in the first place. He felt it had been almost preordained. *I'm surprised she even bothered talking to me on that train,* he thought. *I must have seemed like a total jerk.*

The flight across the continent turned out to be uneventful, though he noticed almost immediately why so many of his friends routinely rave about JetBlue. He enjoyed all the DirecTV channels on the back of the seat in front of him, but it was the service and attitude that made the big difference. Everyone from the check-in agents to the flight attendants to even the pilots seemed proud and honored to be working there. The airline had had a mini-meltdown a few years previously when bad winter weather had strained so many takeoffs and landings, but they managed the PR debacle so effectively that in the end, they managed to gain even more "raving fans." This was customer recovery strategy at its best!

Ari had heard it dozens of times: a company's approach to overcoming a mistake is so critical to recovery that it sometimes actually attracts *new* customers. The really successful hotels, restaurants, airlines, retail stores, and other service entities rely on those strategies all the time—just in case there is a product defect, service error, or poor customer experience.

Applying Guest Recovery Strategies

1. Pay focused and complete attention to the guest.
2. Use principles of active listening.
3. Apologize in a personal and sincere manner.
4. Explain your corrective action. (If not acceptable to the guest, ask what corrective action he or she might prefer.)
5. Depending upon the situation, discuss with your supervisor.
6. Implement a course of action as soon as possible.
7. Offer something of added value with compliments of management for the inconvenience.
8. Thank the guest again for his or her understanding.

Cora gave Ari detailed logistical instructions to get to the hotel once he arrived in Oakland. Everything went smoothly until he got off at the BART station at Montgomery Street. He consulted his map and saw that he was only a few blocks from Nob Hill, where the hotel was located—but what a hill it was! He summoned every ounce of strength he could to pull his overloaded suitcase up the hill to the front steps of the Hotel Metronome. He felt he had come home, somehow.

"Good afternoon, sir," the bellman said as he made his approach. "I always give special credit to people who walk up that hill with a suitcase. Let me help you with your bag, and we'll get you checked in."

"Thank you. I'm here to see an old friend who works at the front desk, so let's surprise her."

"Oh my gosh, are you Cora's New York pal? She is so excited about seeing you again. Come on in. I'm the Damien that she's probably told you horrible things about. But everything is arranged for you. Wait 'til you see the spread they're preparing for the *seder* tonight. Cora is going to pass out when she sees you. She's been beside herself in anticipation."

Cora was in the side office when Ari and Damien strolled up to the front desk, so Tim Olmos quickly notified her that Ari had arrived. She nearly jumped over the desk to embrace him.

"I can't believe you're here, sweetie," Cora said. "I just read a magazine article that you're not even supposed to fly on the High Holy Days."

"Well, technically that's true, but most of the holy days are about being with friends, and I'm not really religious anyway, so I think I will be forgiven. My mother wasn't thrilled about it, though."

Cora introduced Ari to everyone whom he had heard so much about. Though it had been over a year since the two had met on the train, the hotel lost not a single key employee in the duration. Cora considered changing jobs during the summer to be closer to her home and the twins, but Ella and Will allowed her a more flexible schedule so she could stay. They knew how valuable she was and how much the customers adored her.

"Now let me see the famous metronomes," Ari said, making his way into the lobby and bar area. He was immediately impressed. "What a cool theme for a hotel, especially since people staying at hotels are often overly concerned about time. Time for a meeting, time for the theater, time to call the family back home, time to check out."

"That's why we call it Tempus Fugit, or Time Flies," Ella said, proud of the still-new restaurant. Ari immediately liked this woman he had heard about for more than a year. She didn't seem like a Cruella at all.

"Ari, it's five o'clock, and we just started wine hour. I'll bet Tim will cover me for a few minutes while we have a glass or two. Tamara might even upgrade us to champagne."

"Just make sure I get some, too," Tim Olmos said offhandedly, elbows on the front desk. Whether he was joking or not was anyone's guess.

Cora steered Ari past the grand piano, past the Art Deco bookcases with their elegant first editions, past the reading desks, past the house phones. They sat down at two of the barstools just in front of the mirrors, where so many guests had sat over the years. In seconds, they were enjoying the hotel's reserve chardonnay.

"I really can't believe I'm here," Ari said. "The hotel is even nicer than I thought it would be."

"You should have seen it during the renovation when all our flaws were exposed," Cora answered. "I hadn't realized until then how down at the heels it looked in the full light of day. Dim lighting can hide a multitude of evils, you know, but I think we were on our way from shabby chic to just plain shabby. Our guests are too nice to say anything as long as their expectations are being met, and I think they were. Sometimes customers can be *too* forgiving."

"Oh, I don't think so, honey. They are pretty vocal at my place, but it's been so much better lately. The money the parent company has spent on upgrading it has really paid off—for all of us. Even my friend Anne has been singing management's praises lately. She had a birthday recently, and the party was in our conference room. Can you believe it? She even brought that crazy parrot of hers and introduced it—I mean him—to all the guests."

"Oh, you should have brought her, Ari. I would love to meet her. Sounds like she has had quite a career epiphany as well."

"That's appropriately religious considering the holiday," Ari said, barely hiding a smirk. "And what's in store for the celebration tonight? I hope Ella hasn't poisoned the food," he joked.

"You are bad to the bone, mister. Ella has totally gotten on board, and I think it's because we all have figured out that she is simply not the same as us. We've been unfair to her. She's actually a very dedicated professional who is a little on the shy side and has some self-esteem issues, like many of us. As we've welcomed her onto the team, we realize that she adds her own value. It might not be the same as ours, but it's genuine in its own way. I think people need to realize that just because some coworkers don't share too much about their personal lives, they still *have* personal lives—often very rich ones, in fact. I feel we all owe Ella a bit of an apology, though it's probably never going to happen. I don't know why people who are totally professional are often seen as 'mechanical.' It's not fair."

The mood had become a bit somber as Ari contemplated what Cora had said to him since they had first become acquainted on the train.

"I know what you mean, sweetie. When I met you last year, I was dealing with the other side of the coin. *Nobody* I was working with was professional. They were all trying to cope with constant fear of the unknown, fear of losing their jobs, fear of people questioning their own motivations. Our guests sensed it and *pounced*, just like children do when they see that their parents are vulnerable.

"I think the one thing that has happened at our hotel that has made the most difference," Ari continued, "is that the staff feels like we have the ability to create our own destinies. One of our room attendants noticed a half dozen empty Diet Coke cans in a guest's trash. The next time that guest was in the hotel, she put four cans on ice in a bucket for his arrival with a note, "Please enjoy these drinks on the house." He was so thrilled. Another attendant noticed a guest's jacket hanging on the back of a chair with a missing button. She took a few minutes to sew a new one on, so she got major points when he checked out."

Empowering Employees, Part 2

One of the best ways to create empowerment is through relating guest stories to each other. Relate stories by

1. identifying customer experience successes;
2. exchanging one story each day with a fellow team member;
3. asking colleagues and friends for their stories;
4. knowing your strengths and applying them where you can make a difference; and
5. realizing empowerment is a key to being in control of your own accountability.

Cora noticed how excited Ari had become talking about the evolution of his job. She could hardly believe it was the same young man she had had a casual conversation with on a packed and slow-moving train.

Ari said, "All our room agents have recently taken the initiative of offering upgraded rooms, when we have them available of course, at a modest increase in price. It's called selling up. We believe it creates added value and empowers our staff—and our guests love it. We are now all sales agents showcasing the hotel's services. We know our features and benefits better than ever, and it makes us look more professional.

"One of the porters decided to apply for a position in our new deli-restaurant," Ari continued, "so he's become an excellent pastry maker. Even my friend Anne discovered some organizational skills when she coordinated the 10K run I told you about. She's been promoted to assistant manager and harasses my lazy butt every day. I guess I'm the only one there who hasn't been able to get ahead. I'm still walking up three flights of stairs to my little *pied-a-terre* in the Village every night."

Cora thought for a moment before responding.

"You can look at it that way if you want, Ari, but I can tell from just these few minutes that you're happier than I've ever seen you. You've found your passion and gotten your mojo back! I think you have come a long way in your own journey, even if your paycheck doesn't reflect it. It's not about that anyway, and you know it. It's about our own intentions, our expectations, our sense of fulfillment. I would say you are much further along in discovering that than you realize. After all, a happy life is as much about enjoying the journey as getting to the destination."

Ari knew that Cora was right, but he needed some time to reflect.

'You know, Cora, what you say about passion is so right on. I happened upon a book recently that talks about the principles of running a good business. The author called it *The Four P's: Passion, People, Promise, and Product,* if I remember correctly. I actually think I was on the verge of losing my passion, and it was manifesting itself in every aspect of my life. The good news is you really *can* get it back. I am living proof.'

The Four Principles of Running a Good Business

Passion—If you don't have it, you better find a way to get it.

People—Hire the best you can and allow them to be who they are.

Promise—Set the bar high and constantly meet, or exceed, expectations.

Product—Consistency and a "no surprises" attitude will have customers coming back again and again.

Cora and Ari saw each other's reflections in the mirror and realized the bond that had grown between them.

"Ari, I am so glad you discovered that. I was worried about you, I really was. Sometimes those business books my husband reads have a lot of wisdom in them."

"Angel, I need to get freshened up if we're going to do the *seder* tonight. Is that still on?"

"Absolutely," Cora replied. "But it's really more of a celebration meal than a traditional *seder.* Ella and the chef have become *kugel* experts. I can't wait to try the brisket they've been marinating for the past day and a half. Why don't you go up to your room and get settled? I get off at six, so we can meet down here at six thirty. My husband, Jason, arranged for a babysitter for the twins so he can come in and meet you too."

"Oh, I can hardly wait to meet the man who swept you off your feet," Ari said, consulting his passkey. "I'm in 820. Isn't that the penthouse floor? You didn't have to do that, Cora."

"It was our pleasure. You should find some nice flowers and an iced bottle of Pacific Echo, my favorite champagne. Just please don't sample too much before dinner."

"I've always been known for my tolerance of alcohol, so not to worry. But please tell me the elevator is working."

"And that would be a yes, Ari. It is. Just like your new attitude."

Questions for Group Discussion

1. Consider your most recent experience with an effective customer recovery strategy. What were the circumstances? If you were to repeat the strategy, what would you change to make it even more effective?

2. Work schedules are often a point of potential conflict. Flexibility in scheduling is often an answer. What are your experiences with managers accommodating individual schedules? How can issues be worked out?

3. "As we've welcomed Ella onto the team, we realize that she adds her own value," Cora says. Comment on the different personalities you have on your own team and how they complement or conflict with one another.

4. Ari states that the one thing he feels has turned his hotel around is that "staff feels like we have the ability to create our own destinies." Comment on what you believe empowerment to be and how it affects team performance.

5. Discuss the topics of "what constitutes a professional attitude," "how to enjoy the 'precious present,'" and "the journey of arriving at goals."

6. Passion is a key to peak performance. In the service industries, it is a critically important ingredient that provides the energy and enthusiasm customers expect to see and experience. Comment on how you believe you show your passion in your work. What about the level of passion you see on your team?

7. A comment was made that people who are totally professional are often seen as "mechanical." To what extent do you think this is true? In today's world, how important is personality in service? Do guests and customers expect it? When is too much personality over the line?

About the Authors

Considered one of the most authoritative voices in the publishing world, **Charles Decker** is an independent consultant to such companies and organizations as *Time* magazine, CourtTV, Peter Senge's Society for Organizational Learning in Boston, and the training guru Price Pritchett's company, Pritchett, Lp in Dallas. He speaks often to human resources and training groups as well as chambers of commerce across the country and writes and is interviewed regularly for a number of business publications around the globe.

A former senior executive at Amazon.com, he is also the former director of Doubleday's Executive Program book club, at the time the largest business book club in the world, where he regularly previewed more than 2,500 manuscripts every year for potential exposure to book club members.

He launched the Readers' Choice column at *Fast Company* magazine in 2005 and has been involved in the business literacy movement, which encourages group reading of business books in corporate settings, for nearly fifteen years.

Charles is the coauthor with Leslie Yerkes of *Beans: Four Principles for Running a Business in Good Times and Bad*—a Bookscan best seller and BookSense 76 choice, now translated into twenty-plus languages—and the author of *Lessons from the Hive: The Buzz on Surviving and Thriving in an Ever-Changing Workplace,* the Burt's Bees story. He divides his time between New York City and Dallas–Fort Worth.

G ene Ference, MS, PhD, is a leadership strategist and internationally known conference speaker. He is president and founder of Ference Leadership and Strategy & Center for Survey Research, which developed the well-known Peak Performance Wheel, a time-tested approach to building service cultures and improving organizational performance.

Gene's background includes faculty lecturer at Cornell University's world-renowned School of Hotel Administration, director of worldwide training and development and director of the Career Development Institute for Hilton International Hotels, and director of global management development for Inter-Continental Hotels. With more than thirty-five years of industry experience, Gene has directly influenced the service cultures of independent lifestyle hotels and resorts, large-scale international hotel companies, and gaming, food service, retail, leisure, and entertainment organizations.

Several of Gene's clients have received such honors as the Malcolm Baldridge National Quality Award, Employer of Choice, Employer of the Year, and *Fortune* magazine's Best 100 Companies to Work For. Such accolades document how clients achieve continuous improvements in product quality, service excellence, and memorable customer experiences to make significant gains in employee satisfaction, guest loyalty, and long-term financial results.

Gene lives in Weston, Connecticut.

Open Book Editions

A Berrett-Koehler Partner

Open Book Editions is a joint venture between Berrett-Koehler Publishers and Author Solutions, the market leader in self-publishing. There are many more aspiring authors who share Berrett-Koehler's mission than we can sustainably publish. To serve these authors, Open Book Editions offers a comprehensive self-publishing opportunity.

A Shared Mission

Open Book Editions welcomes authors who share the Berrett-Koehler mission—Creating a World That Works for All. We believe that to truly create a better world, action is needed at all levels—individual, organizational, and societal. At the individual level, our publications help people align their lives with their values and with their aspirations for a better world. At the organizational level, we promote progressive leadership and management practices, socially responsible approaches to business, and humane and effective organizations. At the societal level, we publish content that advances social and economic justice, shared prosperity, sustainability, and new solutions to national and global issues.

Open Book Editions represents a new way to further the BK mission and expand our community. We look forward to helping more authors challenge conventional thinking, introduce new ideas, and foster positive change.

For more information, see the Open Book Editions website:
http://www.iuniverse.com/Packages/OpenBookEditions.aspx

Join the BK Community! See exclusive author videos, join discussion groups, find out about upcoming events, read author blogs, and much more! http://bkcommunity.com/